HAL LEONARD

UKULELE METHOD

UKULELE FOR TEENS

A Fun Method Using Songs from Today's Top Artists

BY ALLI JOHNSON & CHAD JOHNSON

To access audio and video, visit:
www.halleonard.com/mylibrary

Enter Code
5769-6258-1114-4747

ISBN 978-1-5400-8800-0

World headquarters, contact:
Hal Leonard
7777 West Bluemound Road
Milwaukee, WI 53213
Email: info@halleonard.com

In Europe, contact:
Hal Leonard Europe Limited
1 Red Place
London, W1K 6PL
Email: info@halleonardeurope.com

In Australia, contact:
Hal Leonard Australia Pty. Ltd.
4 Lentara Court
Cheltenham, Victoria, 3192 Australia
Email: info@halleonard.com.au

INTRODUCTION

Why do we love the ukulele? It's got a great sound, it's portable, and just as importantly, it's an instrument that can be played and enjoyed by people of all ages. The great news is there are even several sizes of ukulele to choose from. The *soprano*—also known as the *standard*—is the smallest of the bunch and a good fit for very young players because of its size. The *concert* is slightly larger than the soprano and is good for young players as well as older players. Next up is the *tenor* ukulele. Many adults tend to prefer this one, as it has a fuller sound and a little more space to fit your fingers onto the fretboard. (A Kremona tenor ukulele was used to record all of the examples in this book.) In another category is the *baritone* ukulele. This one is tuned differently than the other three, so the chords that we use in this book won't apply to the baritone ukulele.

The songs we've selected are some of the most popular pop and rock songs over the last few years that also happen to sound great on the ukulele. Nearly all of the lessons are aimed at teaching you the skills needed to play a specific song. However, by learning the chords, strumming patterns, and fingerpicking patterns in this book, you'll be able to play many more songs as well. We hope you expand your chord library, learn some new techniques, and, most importantly, have fun!

ABOUT THE AUDIO AND VIDEO

Throughout this book, we use a lot of examples to help teach the concepts. Almost all of these examples are demonstrated on the accompanying videos and audio tracks. All examples and songs from the book that appear in the videos are marked with a video icon (), while anything that includes audio will be marked with an audio icon (). You can access these audio and video files by looking on page 1 (title page) for the box with the 16-digit code that says "ENTER CODE." Go to *www.halleonard.com/mylibrary* and enter this code to stream and/or download the audio and video files.

These are really great tools and should definitely be used along with the text and music. It's one thing to understand the concepts on paper, but it's another thing to actually see and/or hear them in action. So be sure to take advantage of these materials!

A QUICK REVIEW

Before we get started, let's quickly review some fundamentals.

PARTS OF THE UKULELE

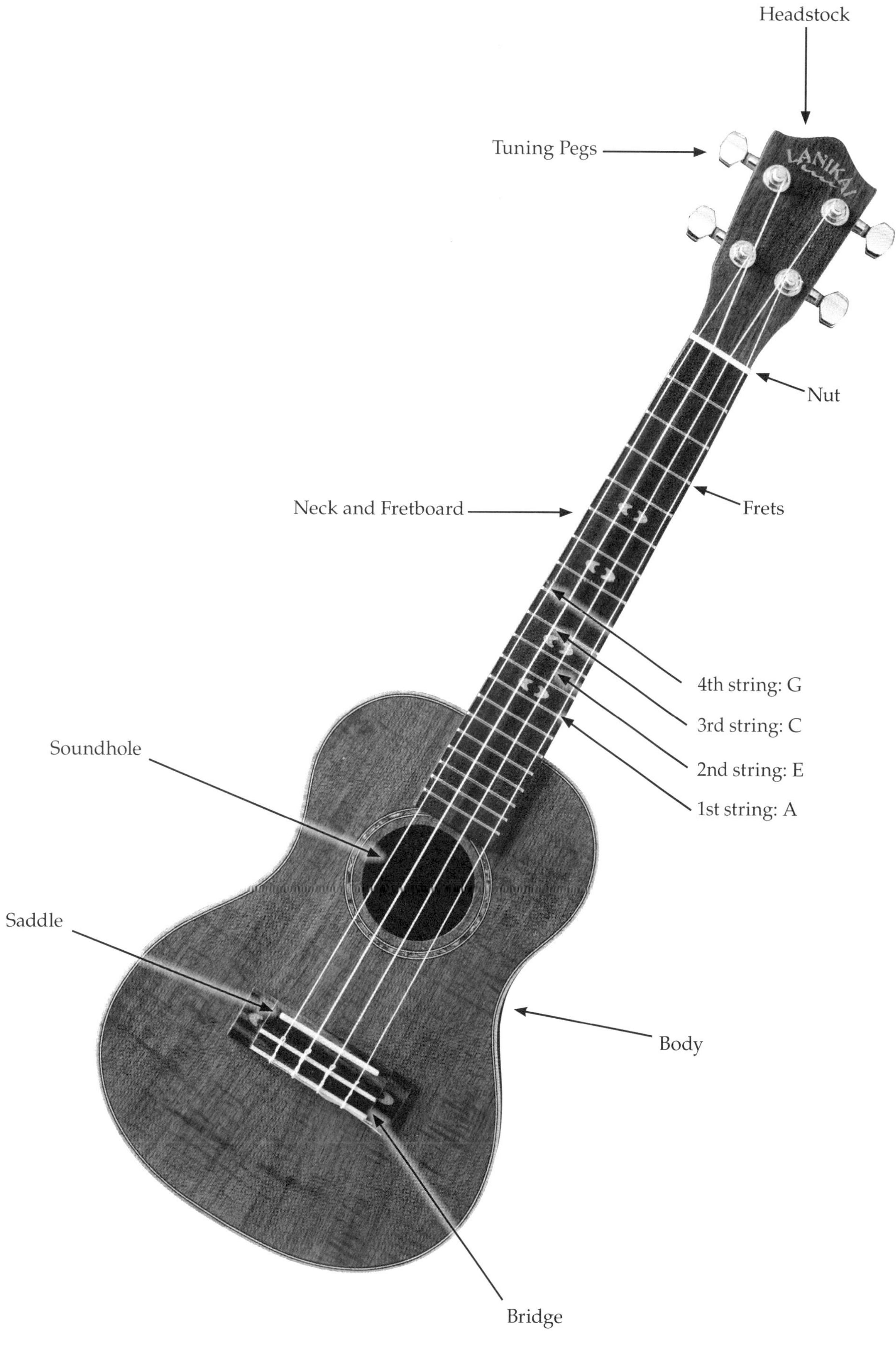

TUNING THE UKULELE

The ukulele is tuned by twisting the tuning pegs on the headstock. When you tighten a tuning peg, the pitch goes up. When you loosen a tuning peg, the pitch goes down.

The ukulele is tuned to the following pitches:

String 1: A

String 2: E

String 3: C

String 4: G

A — 1st string
E — 2nd string
C — 3rd string
G — 4th string

Electronic Tuners

An electronic tuner is really helpful when you're starting out. It will "listen" to your strings and tell you whether they are *sharp* (too high) or *flat* (too low). A clip-on tuner is especially handy because you can leave it clipped to your headstock.

Tuning to the Audio 

If you don't have an electronic tuner, you can use the accompanying audio to tune. We'll give you the tuning pitches for each string three times.

STRETCHING OUT

New ukulele strings can sometimes take a while to stretch out. This means that when you get a new ukulele—or put new strings on your ukulele—you may have to retune it many times before it begins to stay in tune. You can usually speed up this process by stretching the strings. Just push each string down with the thumb while pulling in the opposite direction with the fingers. Do this several times on each string. This should help the uke stay in tune much more quickly!

Tuning to a Piano

If you have a piano or keyboard nearby, you can use it to tune your ukulele. Match the open strings to the following pitches:

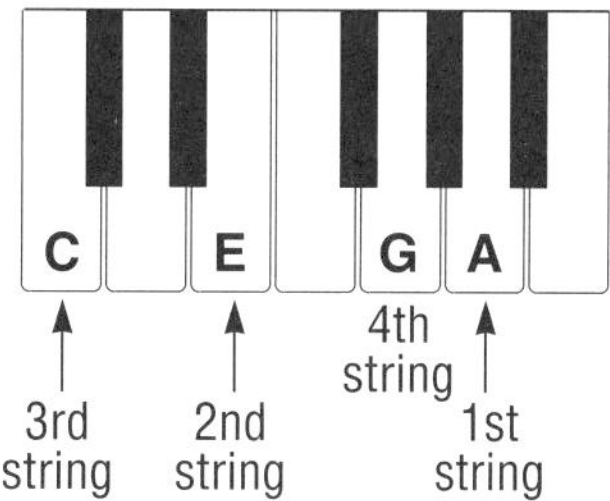

MUSIC READING BASICS

Pitch

Music notes are a written on a *staff,* which has five *lines* and four *spaces* (in between the lines). Notes get higher in pitch as they move up the staff and lower in pitch as they move down. A *clef* sits at the beginning of a staff and tells you which notes are assigned to the lines and spaces. Ukulele music uses the *treble clef.*

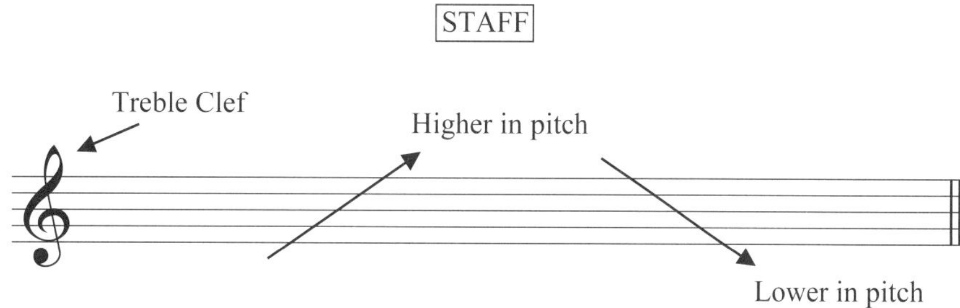

Each line and space is given a note from the *music alphabet*, which includes the letters A through G. The lines, from low to high, are E–G–B–D–F, as in **E**very **G**ood **B**oy **D**oes **F**ine. The spaces, F–A–C–E, spell the word "face."

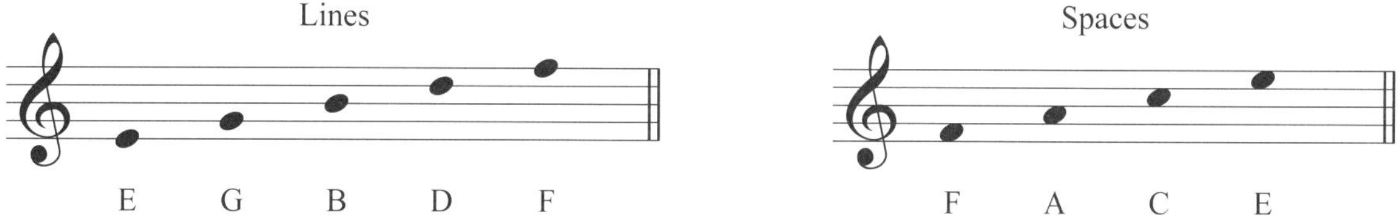

Measures and Bar Lines

Bar lines divide the music into *measures* (or *bars*), which makes it easier to keep your place in the music. A *double bar line* is used to mark the end of a section or the end of a song.

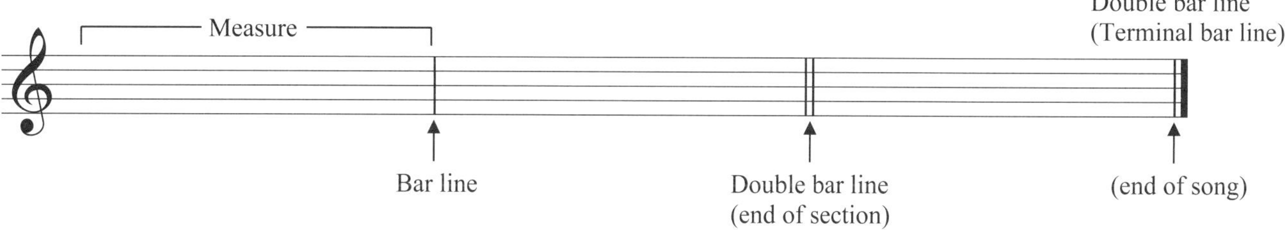

Rhythm

Each measure contains a number of *beats*. The beat is what you tap your foot to when you hear music. A *time signature*—two numbers, one on top of the other—appears at the beginning of a piece of music and tells you how these beats are organized. 4/4 is the most common time signature.

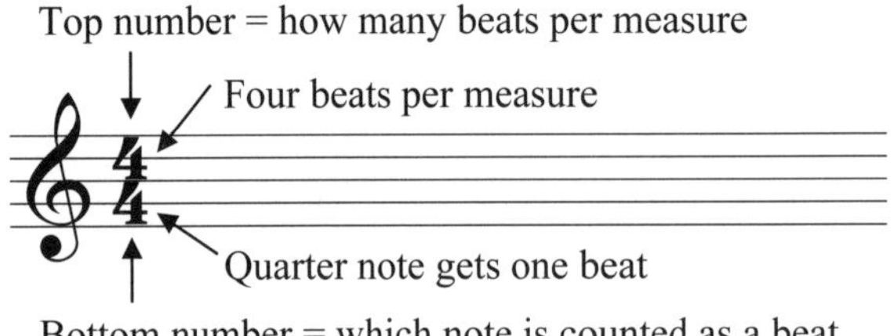

Along with pitch (the highness or lowness), each note has a rhythm as well. This tells you how long (how many beats) each note sounds.

- A **whole note** 𝅝 lasts 4 beats.
- A **half note** 𝅗𝅥 lasts 2 beats.
- A **quarter note** ♩ lasts 1 beat.

Chord Grids

A *chord* is three or more notes played at the same time. We strum chords on the ukulele to play songs. *Chord grids* show how to play them. The vertical lines represent the strings, and the horizontal lines represent the frets. Dots on the grid show you where to put your fingers. The fingers of your fretting hand are numbered 1 through 4.

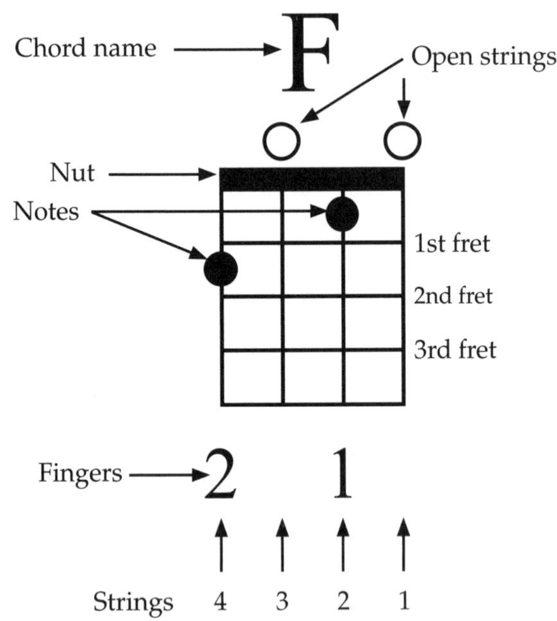

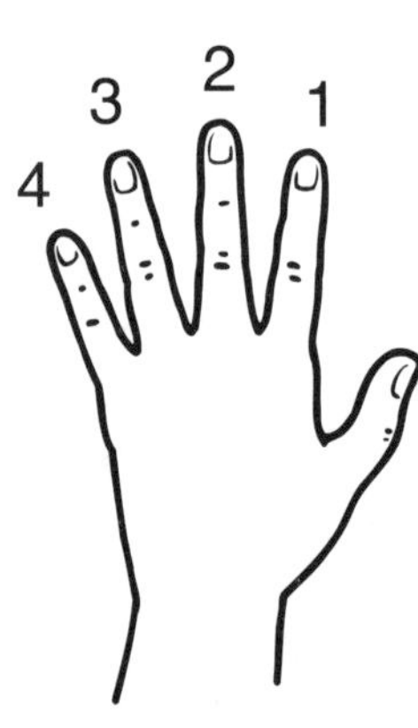

Fretting hand

CHAPTER 1: YOUR FIRST CHORDS

Let's get started with a few common chords on the ukulele. Remember, a chord is simply several notes played at the same time. Chords create the harmony in a song.

C CHORD

First up is a *C major chord*, and it's a simple one. Just place your third finger on fret 3 of string 1.

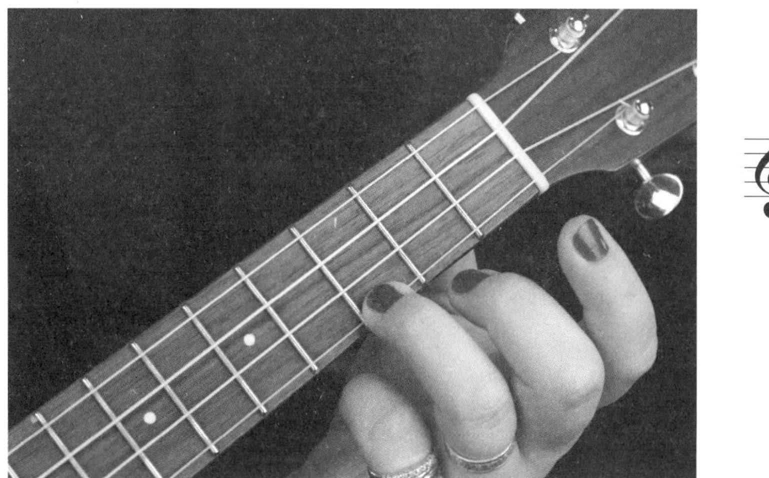

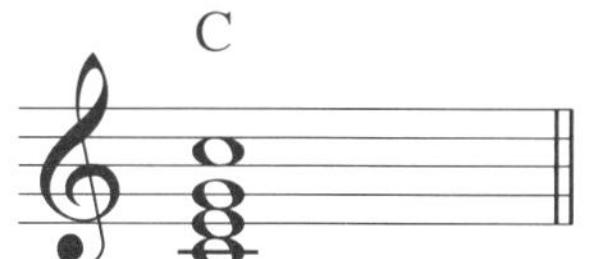

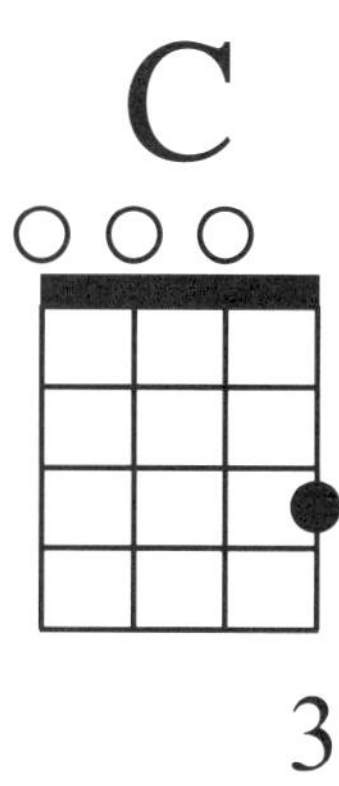

Am CHORD 

"Am" is short for "A minor." This is a *minor chord*. Where major chords sound happy or bright, minor chords sound sad or dark. For Am, just place your second finger on fret 2 of string 4.

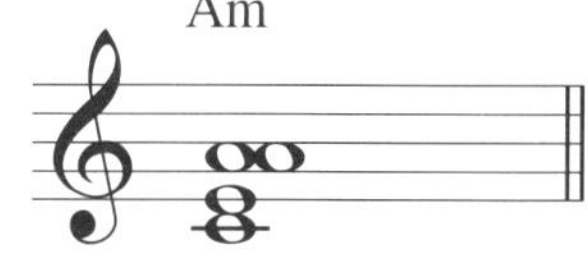

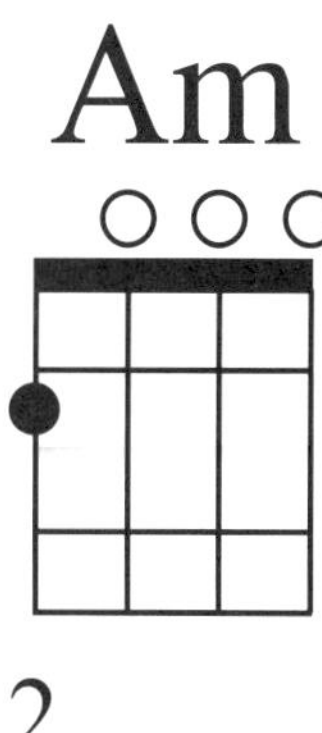

IMPORTANT!

When you learn a new chord, pluck each string separately to make sure that every note is ringing clearly. If a string sounds muffled or buzzy, adjust your fingers until all the strings are ringing clearly.

Exercise 1

Let's try switching between the two chords now. We'll strum down with our thumb once for each chord, holding each for four beats. These are whole notes. Count aloud from one to four for each chord.

RHYTHM NOTATION

When strumming chords, we'll use rhythm notation as a shorthand. Instead of writing all the notes in the chord, we'll show the chord name and then use diamond- and slash-shaped notes to show the rhythm:

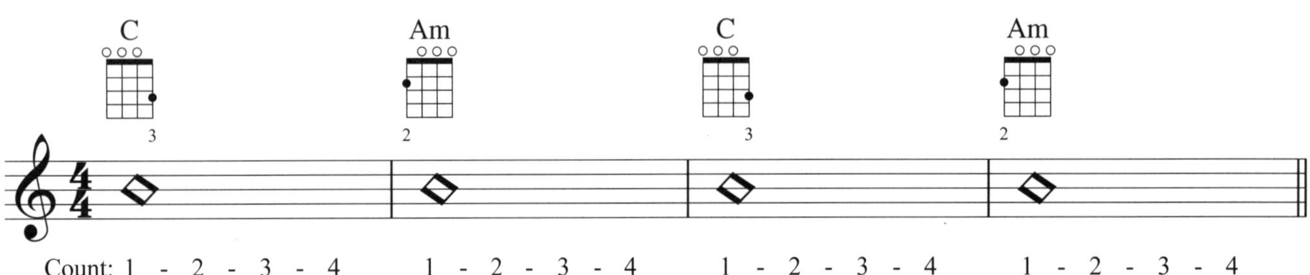

Exercise 2

Now let's try a quicker change between the two chords. Each chord will be held for two beats, so we'll be playing half notes. The *close repeat sign* :‖ at the end tells you to go back to the *open repeat sign* ‖: at the beginning and play the example again.

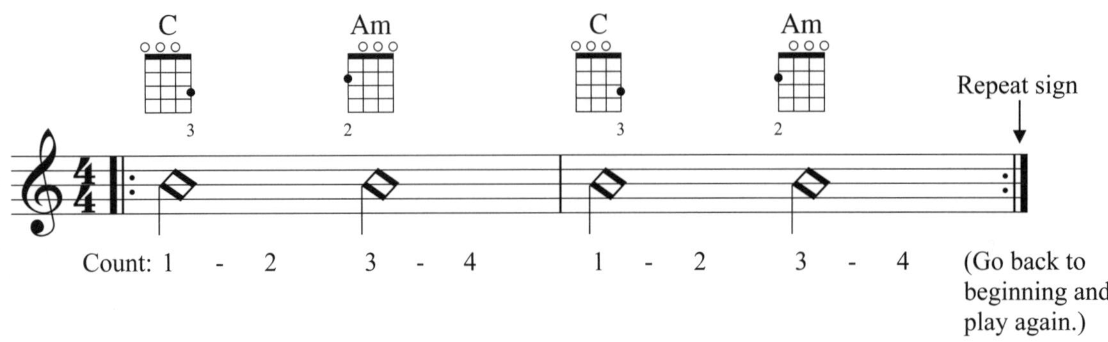

F CHORD

Let's add another chord now. This is an F major chord, and it's like your Am chord, but you also add your first finger on fret 1 of string 2.

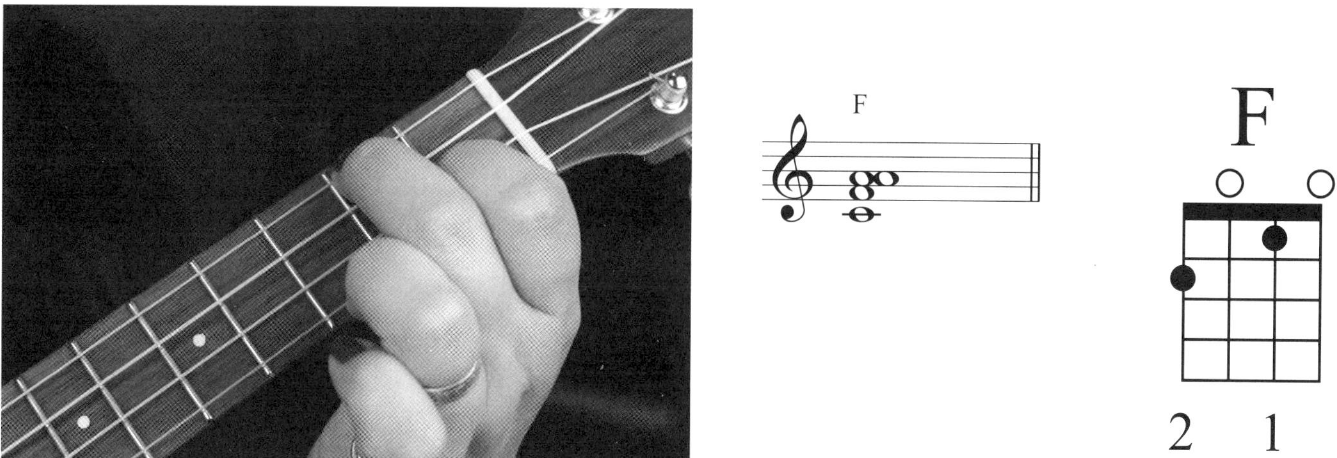

Exercise 3

Let's use the F chord with the other two chords. First, we'll switch between Am and F. We'll strum once on every beat here, or in quarter notes.

IMPORTANT!

When switching between Am and F, keep your second finger down on fret 2 of string 4 the whole time. Just add your first finger for the F chord and lift it off for the Am chord.

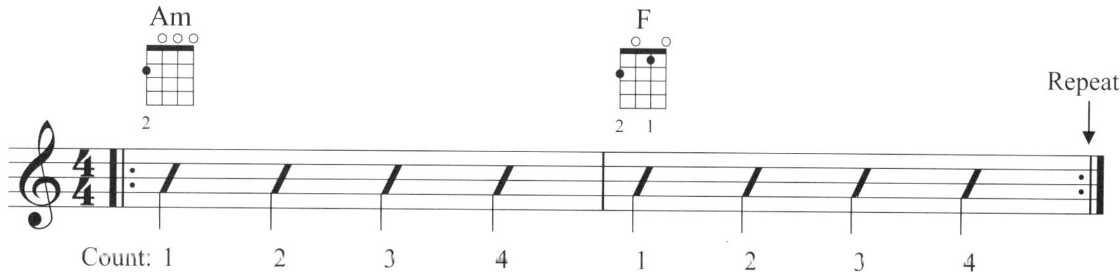

Exercise 4

And now let's switch between C and F. Try to see the F chord in your mind while still playing the C chord.

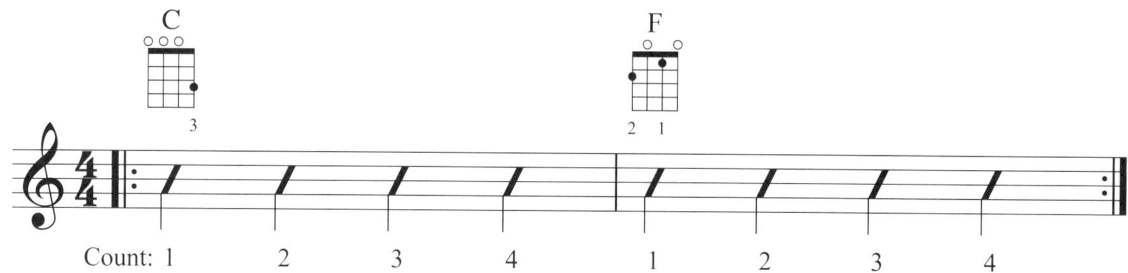

Guess what? You know enough chords for your first song! Using our three chords—C, Am, and F—we're going to play the chorus from "Lost Boy" by Ruth B.

A NOTE ABOUT THE SONG MELODIES

Even though we are focusing on playing the chords and accompaniment, we have also included the song melodies for reference and for those who are already skilled at reading standard music notation.

LOST BOY

Words and Music by Ruth Berhe

Am
C
F
"Run, run, lost boy," they say to me,
C
Am
C
"a - way from all of
F
C
re - al - i - ty."
Am
C
sim.
Nev - er - land is home to the lost boys like me; and
F
C
Am
lost boys like me are free. Nev - er - land is home to the
C
F
C
lost boys like me; and lost boys like me are free.

G CHORD

Let's add one more chord in this chapter: a G major chord. We're using three fingers on this one, so it's a bit more challenging.

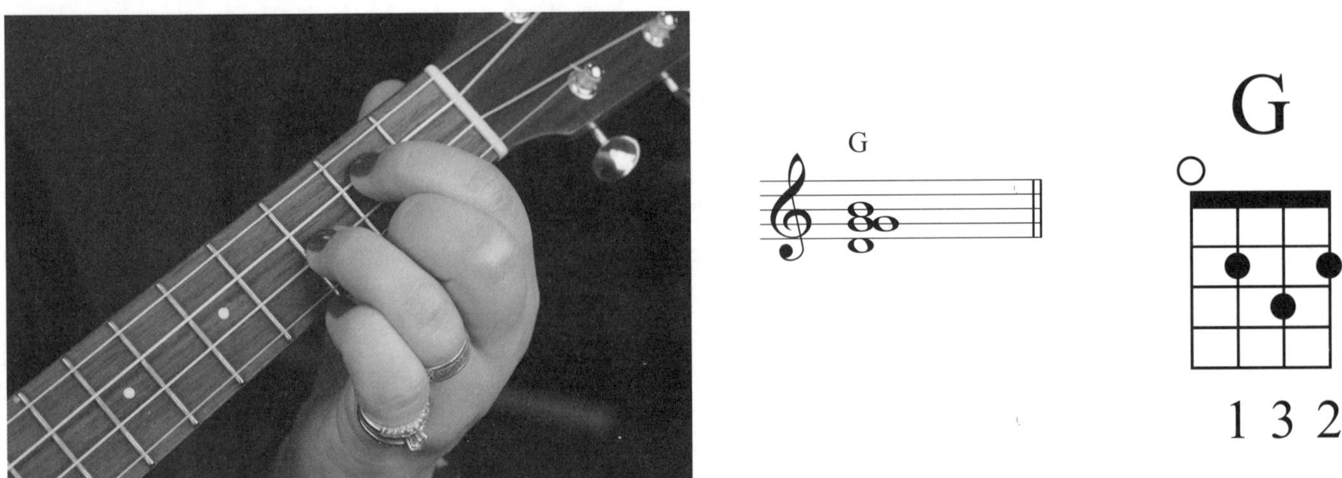

KEEP 'EM TRIMMED!

In chords like G major, where you're using several fingers at once, you need to keep your fingers arched so that they aren't touching other strings accidentally. In order to do this, you need to keep your fingernails trimmed so they're not getting in the way.

Exercise 5

Let's make use of our G chord now and alternate it with Am. We'll play two quarter notes and one half note in each measure.

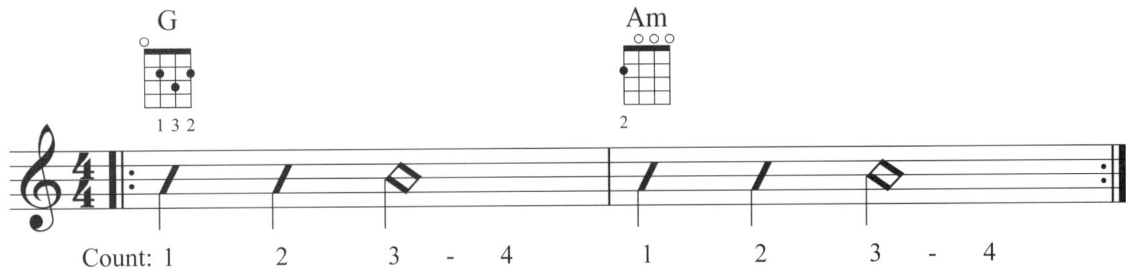

Exercise 6

Now let's move back and forth between F and G chords in half notes. We'll strum once for each chord and hold it for two beats.

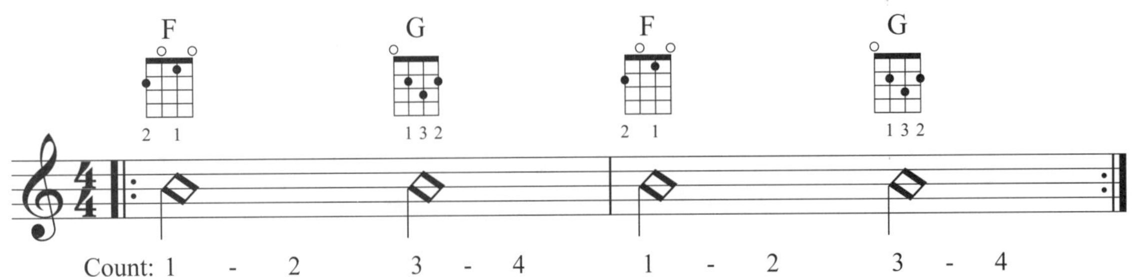

MUSCLE MEMORY

It may seem almost impossible at first to change quickly between chords—especially with a chord like G that uses three fingers. But if you stick with it, we promise it will get easier! You will develop muscle memory, and in time, your fingers will learn to go right where they need to go without even thinking about it. It just takes a bit of practice!

Exercise 7

Finally, let's switch between C and G chords. We'll strum in straight quarter notes here.

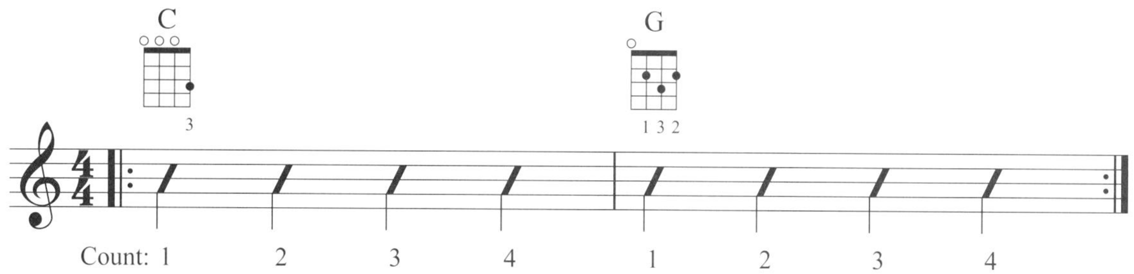

CHORD NAMES AND SYMBOLS

The letters you see above the chord grids—like C, G, Am, etc.—are called the *chord symbols*, and they're a shorthand for the *chord names*. An uppercase letter by itself (C, G, F) stands for a major chord. For a minor chord, the chord symbol will have a suffix of "m" after the uppercase letter (Am). So:

- C = C major chord
- F = F major chord
- G = G major chord
- Am = A minor chord

Let's close out this chapter with another song. With our C, Am, F, and G chords, we can play Taylor Swift's "Love Story."

FIRST AND SECOND ENDINGS

In "Love Story," we have a new kind of repeat called *first and second endings*. First, you play until you reach the close repeat sign (:‖), which appears at the end of the first ending bracket. Then you go back to the open repeat sign (‖:) and start playing from there again. This time, you skip over the first ending bracket and go to the second ending bracket.

LOVE STORY

Words and Music by Taylor Swift

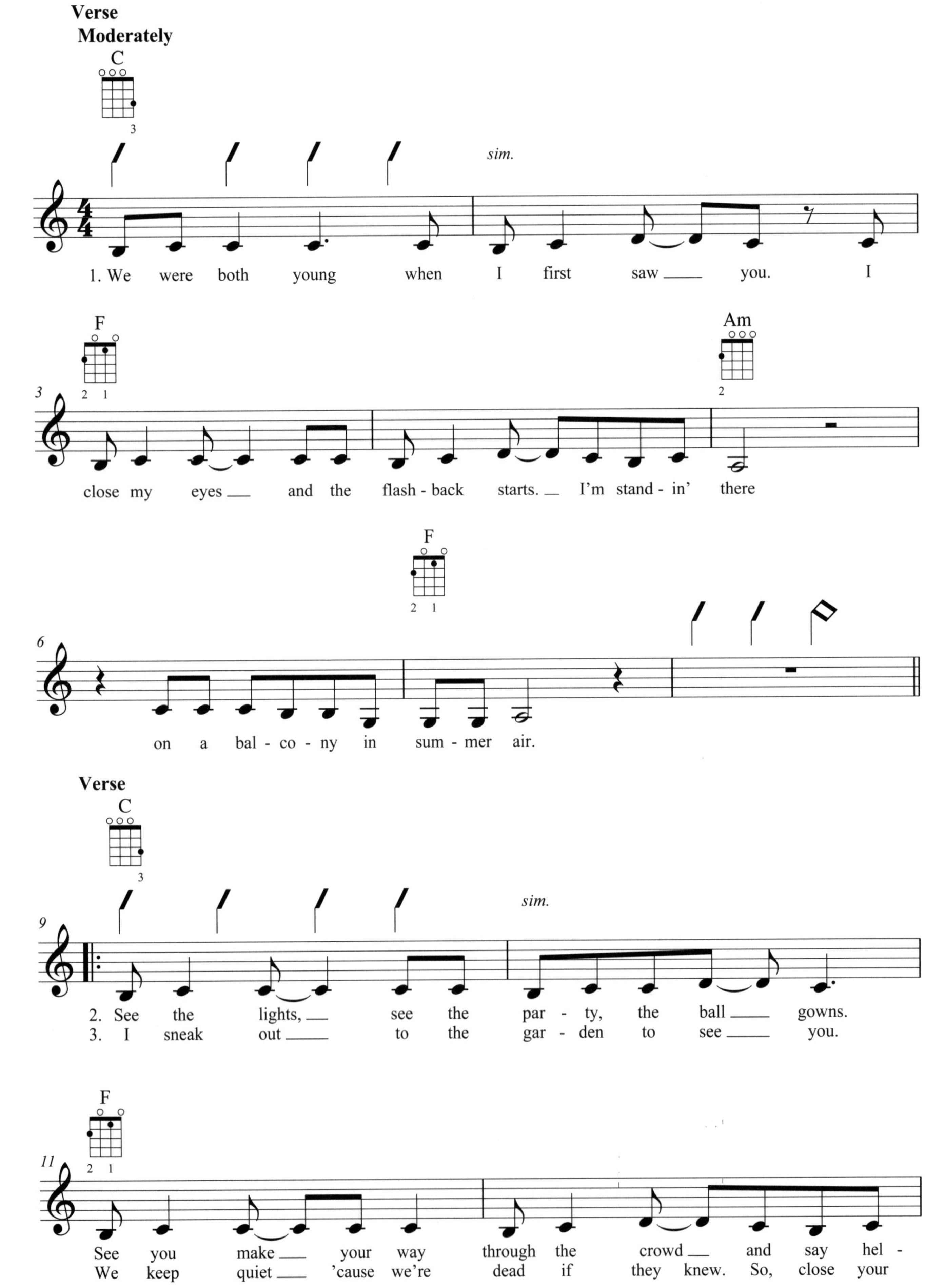

Verse
Moderately

C

sim.

1. We were both young when I first saw __ you. I

F Am

3 close my eyes __ and the flash - back starts. __ I'm stand - in' there

F

6 on a bal - co - ny in sum - mer air.

Verse

C

sim.

9 2. See the lights, __ see the par - ty, the ball __ gowns.
3. I sneak out __ to the gar - den to see __ you.

F

11 See you make __ your way through the crowd __ and say hel -
We keep quiet __ 'cause we're dead if they knew. So, close your

Am
G
13
lo. Lit - tle did I ___ know
eyes, es - cape this town for a lit - tle while.
F
16
that you were Ro - me - o. You were
'Cause you were Ro - me - o. I was the
G
Am
18
throw - ing peb - bles, and my dad - dy said, "Stay a - way from
scar - let let - ter, and my dad - dy said, "Stay a - way from
C
F
20
Ju - li - et." ___ And I was cry - in' on the stair - case,
Ju - li - et." ___ But you were ev - 'ry - thing to me. I was
G
Am
22
beg - gin' you, "Please ___ don't go." ___
Chorus
F
G
C
sim.
24
And I ___ said, "Ro - me - o, take me some-where we can be a - lone.

CHAPTER REVIEW

Here's what we learned in this chapter:

- Four chords: **C, Am, F,** and **G**.
- **Major chords** sound happy or bright. **Minor chords** sound sad or dark.
- In **chord symbols**, an uppercase letter by itself stands for a major chord. An uppercase letter with an "m" suffix stands for a minor chord.
- Two songs: **"Lost Boy"** and **"Love Story."**
- When you learn a new chord, **pluck each string to make sure all the notes are clear**.
- Keep the fingernails on your fretting hand trimmed.
- The more you practice, the easier playing chords will be!
- **First and second endings** are a new kind of repeat where you play the first ending the first time through and the second ending the second time through.

CHAPTER 2: BASIC STRUM PATTERNS

Now that you have a few chords under your fingers, let's try learning some common strum patterns. (We'll learn a few more chords as well.) Songs often have a unique rhythmic feel, and different strum patterns help us achieve this on the uke.

A BIT ABOUT STRUMMING TECHNIQUE

In Chapter 1, we started off by strumming down with our thumb for each chord. This is always an option, and it sounds especially nice on ballads. However, most people strum more active patterns on the uke with their index finger.

To do this, form the index finger into a loose hook shape and lightly brace the crease of its first joint (nearest the tip) with the thumb. Curl the remaining three fingers loosely into the palm (see photos).

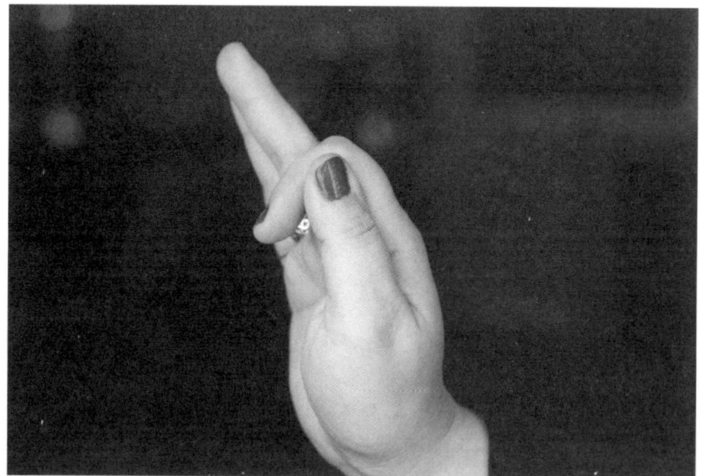

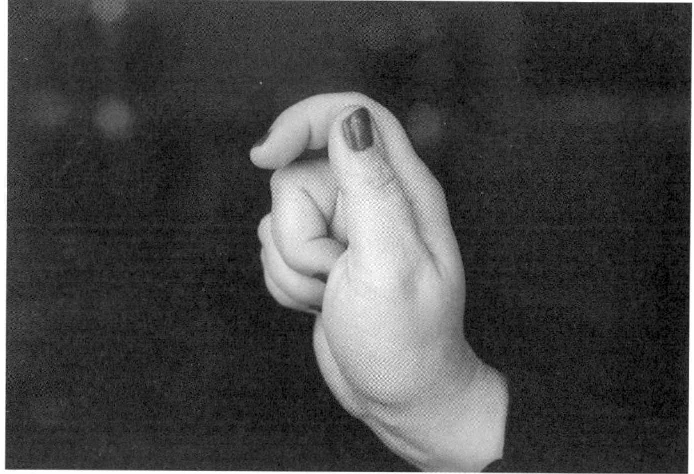

Most people prefer to strum the strings close to where the body meets the neck. There are two reasons for this:

1. It produces a nice, balanced tone.
2. The string tension is less here than it is over the soundhole, and therefore it's easier for the finger to glide through the strings.

Try using this basic technique for the examples in this chapter. It's good to become comfortable with both thumb- and index-finger strumming, as they both have uses.

USING ACCENTS

The first pattern we're going to look at isn't really a new pattern at all; in fact, we played it in Chapter 1. However, now we're going to make it *sound* new by using a concept called *accents*. Simply put, an accented strum is one that's a bit louder than the other strums around it. Using accents can help the music come alive.

To demonstrate, let's listen to the same strum pattern—straight quarter notes—on a C chord. The first time, we'll play it with no accents. Then, we'll play it with an accent (>) on beats 2 and 4, and we'll officially call this Strum Pattern 1.

Exercise 1

Without Accents

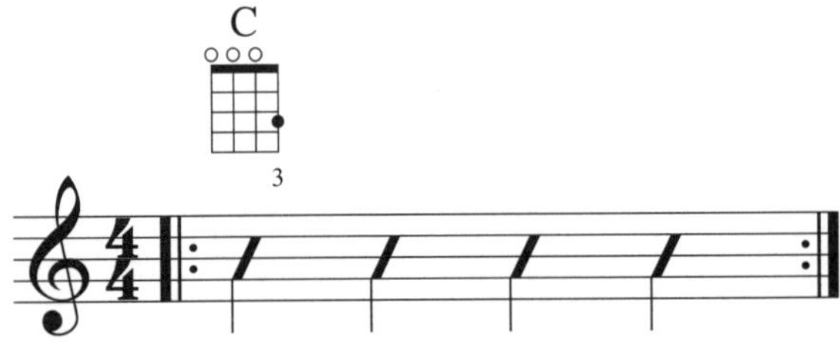

With Accents: Strum Pattern 1

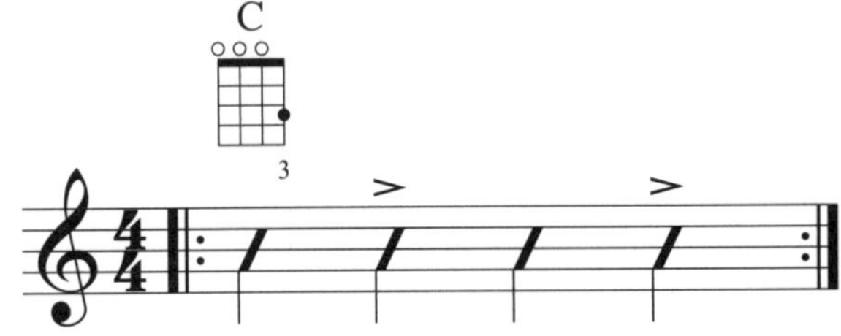

Notice how the accents make the pattern suddenly come alive and start to sound like actual music!

HERE, THERE, AND EVERYWHERE!

Try listening to your favorite songs and see if you can spot some accents. Once you know what to listen for, you'll hear them popping out all over the place. The truth is that many performers use accents without realizing it, because they learned them by listening to and imitating *their* favorite performers when they started out. Accents are an important part of musical *dynamics* (that is, playing some notes loudly and others softly), which help music to breathe and sound more human.

Now let's try using Strum Pattern 1 (quarter notes with accents on beats 2 and 4) on a chord progression: C–G–Am–F.

Exercise 2

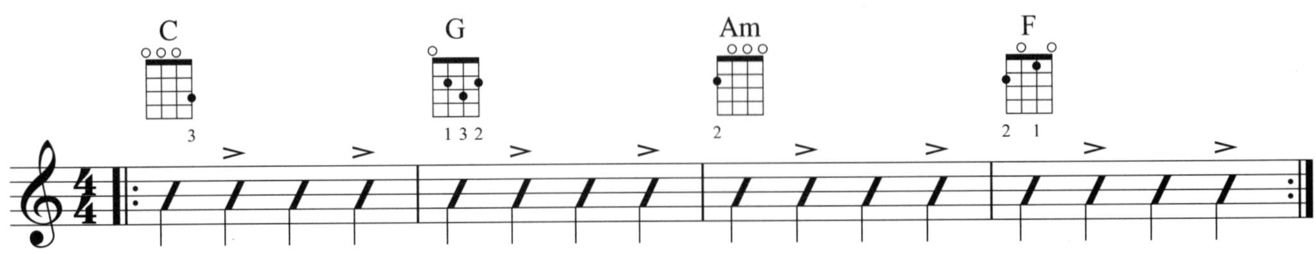

THE BACKBEAT

Beats 2 and 4 are known as the *backbeat*. Accenting these beats in a strum pattern kind of simulates the snare drum in a drum beat, as the snare is usually played on beats 2 and 4 in a typical beat.

ADDING EIGHTH NOTES

We've played whole notes (four beats), half notes (two beats), and quarter notes (one beat) in our strums so far, but now it's time to try some *eighth notes*. When an eighth note appears by itself, it has a *flag* ♪. Two or more consecutive eighth notes are *beamed* together ♫.

An eighth note gets half a beat, so there are two of them for every quarter note. We count them by adding an "and" (&) between the beat numbers.

When we strum in eighth notes, we usually alternate strumming down and up. You'll strum down on the beat numbers (the *downbeats*) and up on the "ands" (or *upbeats*) between them.

⊓ = downstrum

V = upstrum

Watch the video and try the following exercises to get the feel of strumming eighth notes. Pay attention to the strum directions. We'll refer to these next two as Strum Pattern 2 and Strum Pattern 3.

Exercise 3: Strum Pattern 2

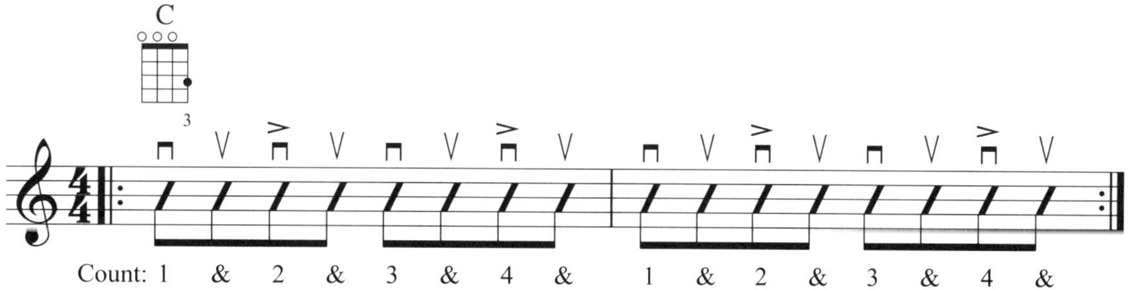

Exercise 4: Strum Pattern 3

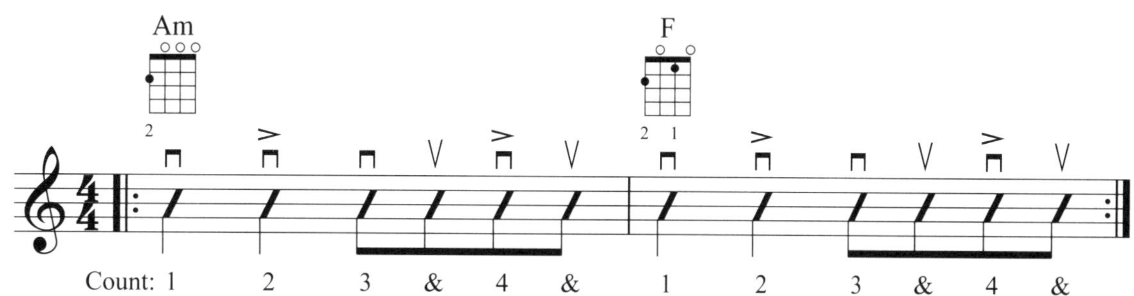

D CHORD

How about a new chord? For a D major chord, place three fingers at fret 2 on the fourth, third, and second strings. Notice there are a couple of fingering options for this one.

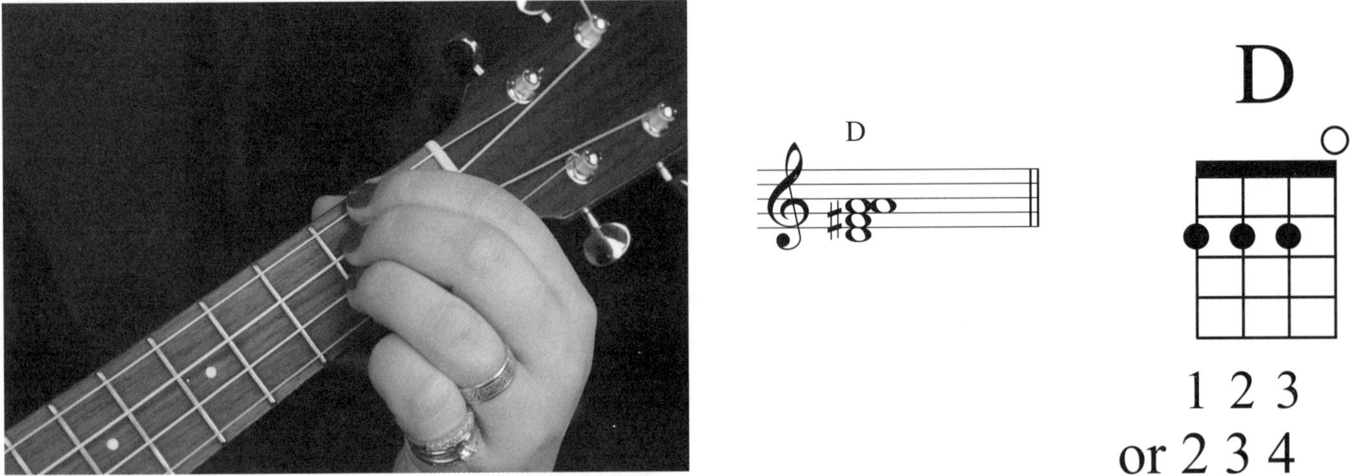

SHUFFLE FEEL

Before we use our new D chord, let's talk about the *shuffle feel.* This is a way of playing eighth notes that sounds a bit lopsided. The notes on the downbeats are longer than the ones on the upbeats.

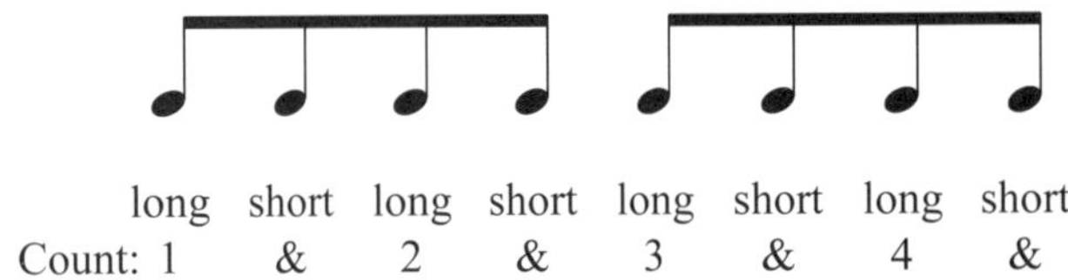

long short long short long short long short
Count: 1 & 2 & 3 & 4 &

It's easier to hear than it is to explain with words, so listen to the audio or watch the video to hear the difference between the normal (or *straight*) feel and the shuffle feel. You'll recognize it right away because you've heard it many times.

Now let's make use of our new D chord and our F chord. We'll use Strum Pattern 3 with a shuffle feel. When a song uses a shuffle feel, you'll usually see one of three things in the written music:

- "Shuffle Feel"
- "Swing Feel"
- This symbol: (♫ = ♩♪ triplet)

They all mean the same thing, and in this book, we'll use (♫ = ♩♪ triplet).

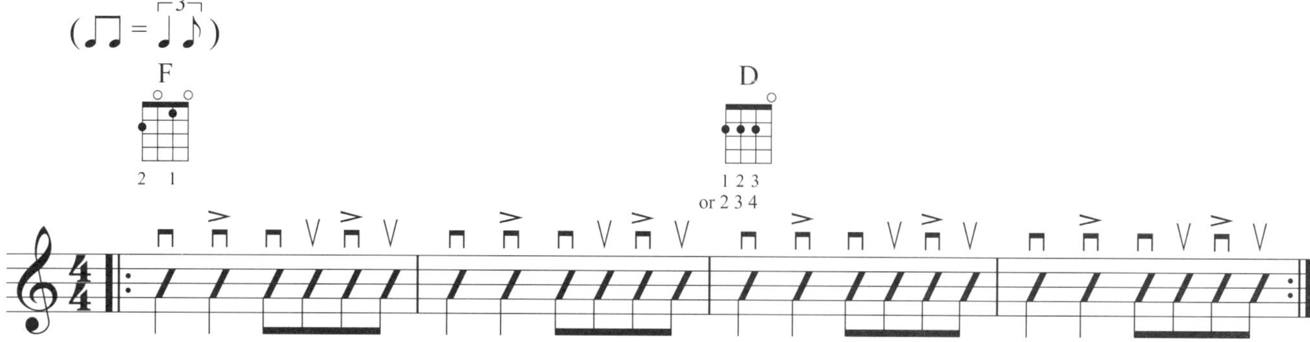

FINGERINGS MATTER!

If you use the alternate fingering shown for the D chord—fingers 2, 3, and 4 instead of fingers 1, 2, and 3—it's much easier to switch from F to D, because you can leave your second finger on string 4 at the second fret the whole time!

Now let's play another song: "I'm Yours" by Jason Mraz. We'll use our new D chord and Strum Pattern 3 with a shuffle feel for most of the song. Don't forget to place those accents on beats 2 and 4 to make it swing even more!

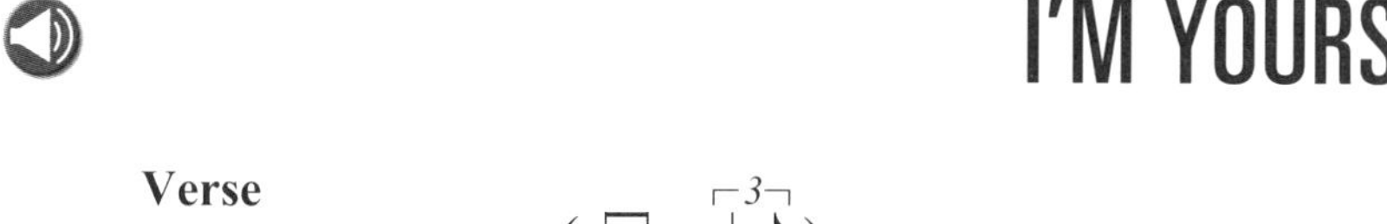

I'M YOURS

Words and Music by Jason Mraz

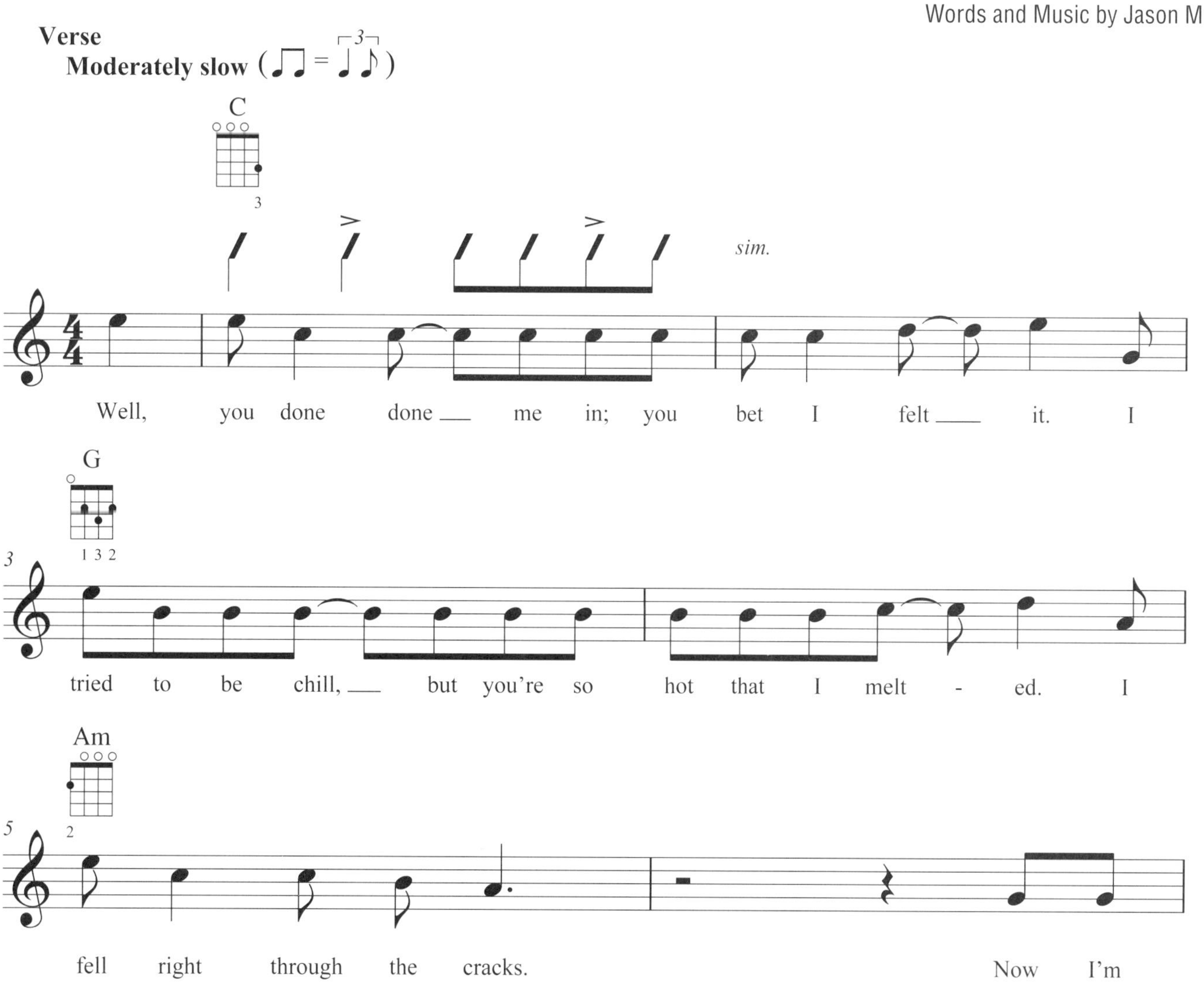

Verse
Moderately slow

C

3

sim.

Well, you done done __ me in; you bet I felt __ it. I

G

1 3 2

3

tried to be chill, __ but you're so hot that I melt - ed. I

Am

2

5

fell right through the cracks. Now I'm

F
7
try - ing to get back.
Be - fore the
C
9
cool done run out, I'll be giv - ing it my best - est, and
G
11
noth - ing's gon - na stop me but di - vine in - ter - ven - tion. I
Am
13
F
reck - on it's a - gain my turn to win some or learn some. But
Chorus
C
G
Am
sim.
17
I won't hes - i - tate no more, no more. This
F
C
sim.
22
can - not wait. I'm yours.

G
Am
F
Verse
C
G
2. Well, o - pen up your mind and see like me. O - pen up your
Am
plans and, damn, you're free. Look in - to your heart and you'll find
F
C
love, love, love, love. Lis - ten to the mu - sic of the
G
mo - ment; peo - ple dance and sing. We're just one big fam - i - ly,
Am
F
and it's our god - for - sak - en right to be loved, loved,

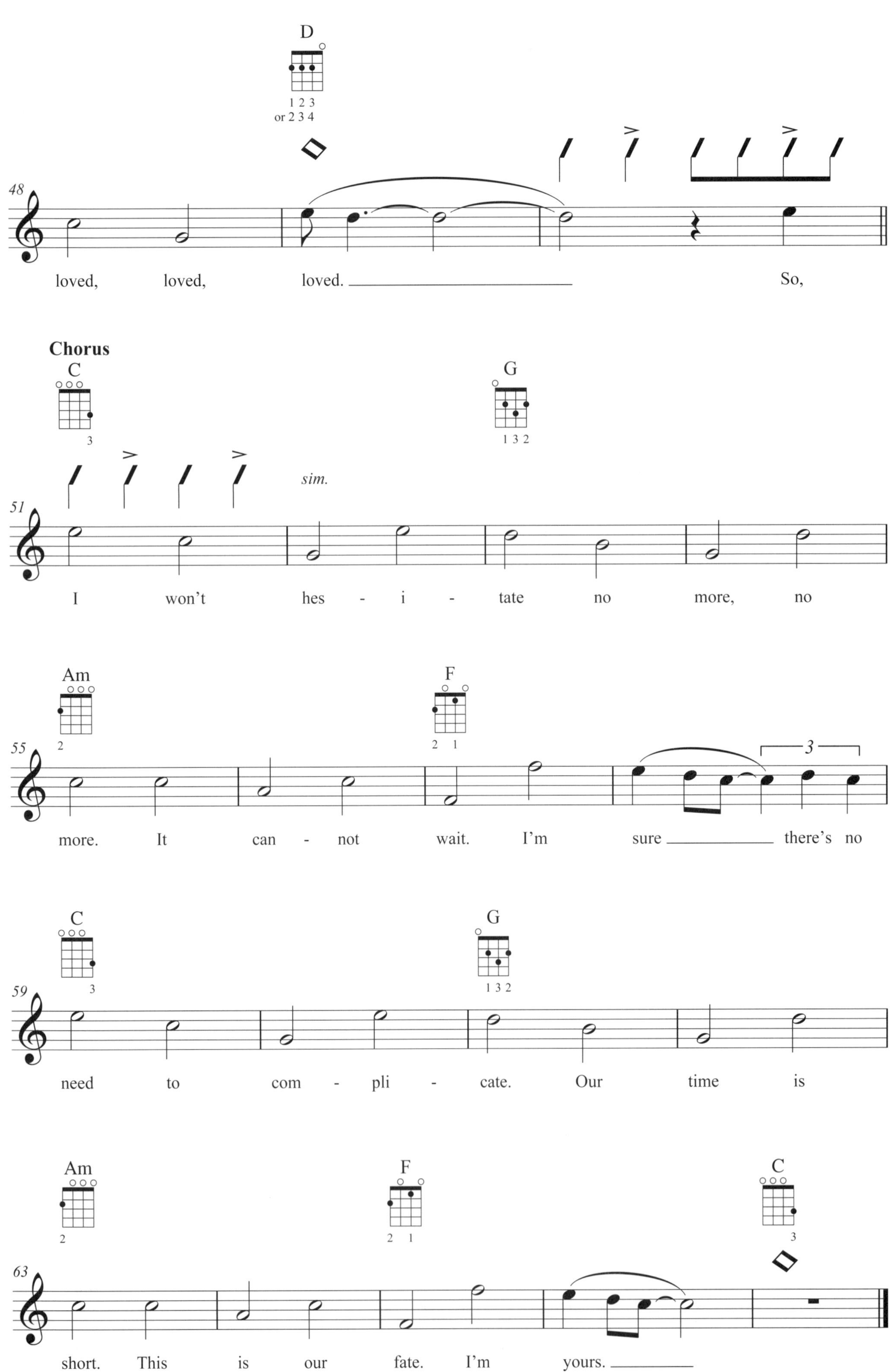
D
1 2 3
or 2 3 4
48
loved, loved, loved. So,
Chorus
C
3
G
1 3 2
sim.
51
I won't hes - i - tate no more, no
Am
2
F
2 1
55
more. It can - not wait. I'm sure there's no
C
3
G
1 3 2
59
need to com - pli - cate. Our time is
Am
2
F
2 1
C
3
63
short. This is our fate. I'm yours.

Em CHORD

It's time to learn your second minor chord: Em.

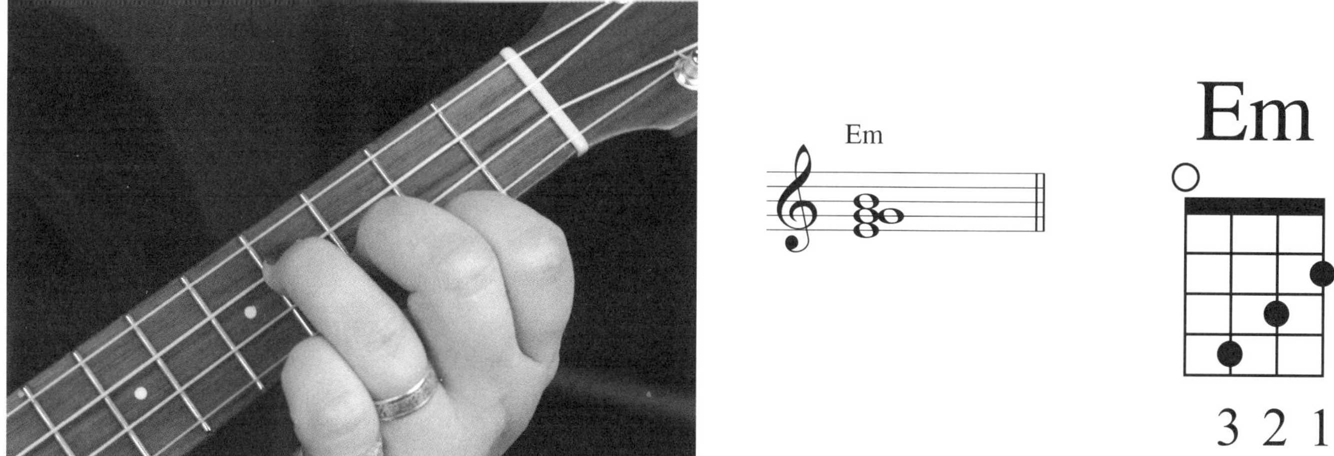

Let's try using Em with some of our other chords now. First, let's use Em and C.

Exercise 6

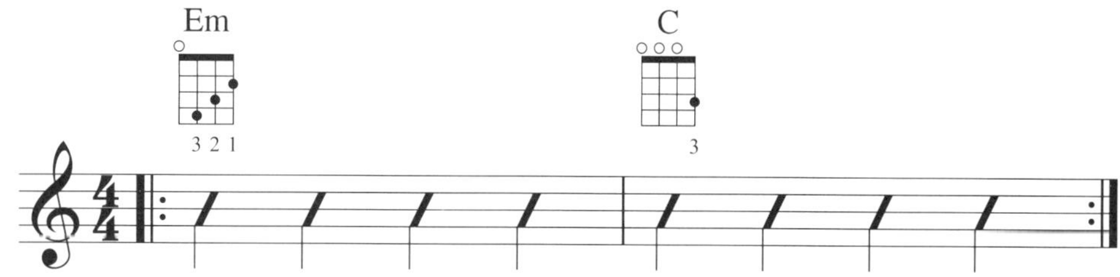

Now we'll play Am and Em using Strum Pattern 2.

Exercise 7

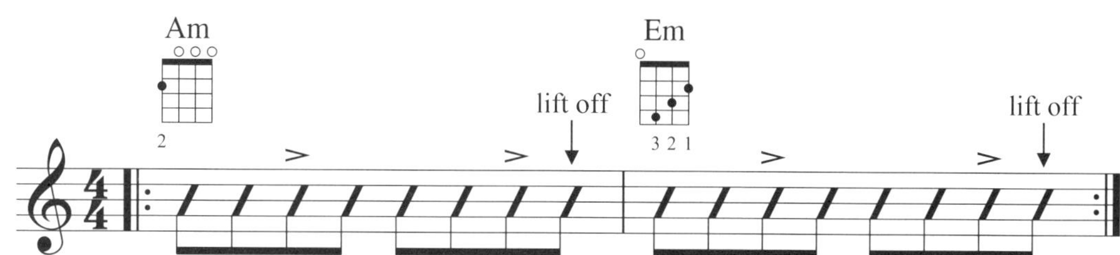

EARLY RELEASE

When you're strumming in eighth notes and have to change between two chords, like Am and Em, you can release your fretting fingers an eighth note early (see Exercise 7). This gives you time to get to the next chord.

Let's use Em in a song. For Katy Perry's "Firework," we'll use G, Am, Em, and C chords with Strum Patterns 2 and 1.

FIREWORK

Words and Music by Katy Perry, Mikkel Eriksen, Tor Erik Hermansen, Esther Dean and Sandy Wilhelm

G
Am
13
Do you know that there's still a chance for you?

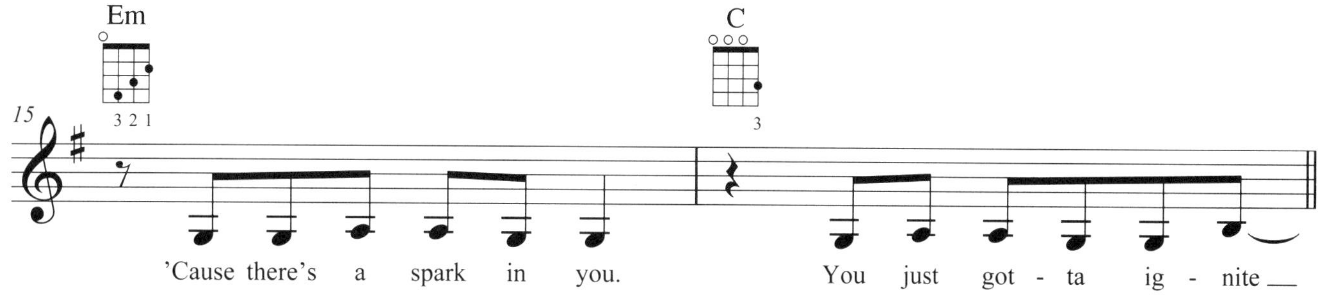
Em
C
15
'Cause there's a spark in you. You just got - ta ig - nite

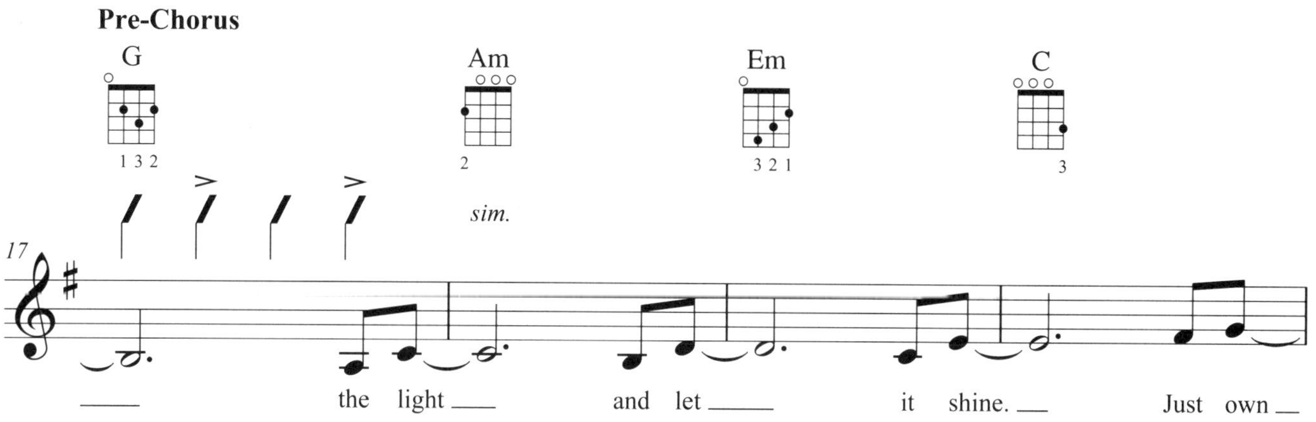
Pre-Chorus
G
Am
Em
C
sim.
17
the light and let it shine. Just own

G
Am
Em
21
the night like the Fourth of Ju - ly.

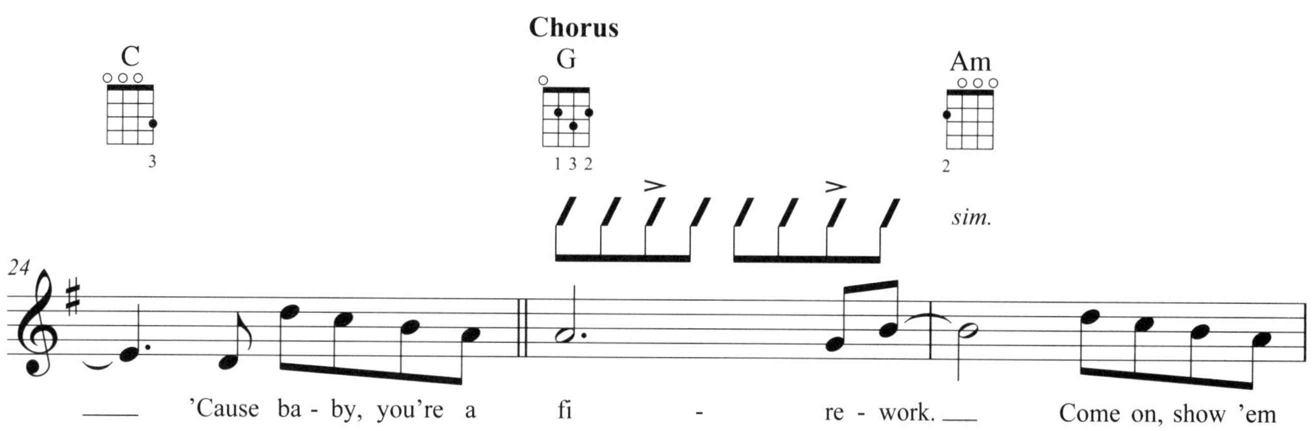
Chorus
C
G
Am
sim.
24
'Cause ba - by, you're a fi - re - work. Come on, show 'em

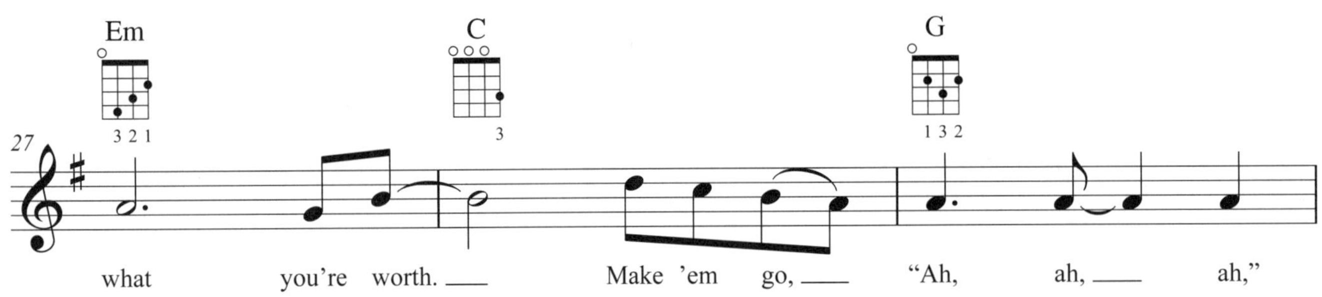
Em
C
G
3 2 1
3
1 3 2
27
what you're worth. Make 'em go, "Ah, ah, ah,"

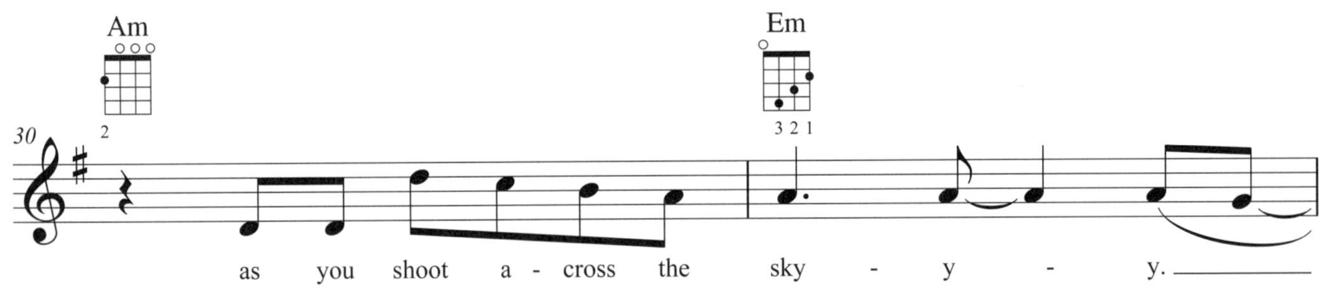
Am
Em
2
3 2 1
30
as you shoot a - cross the sky - y - y.

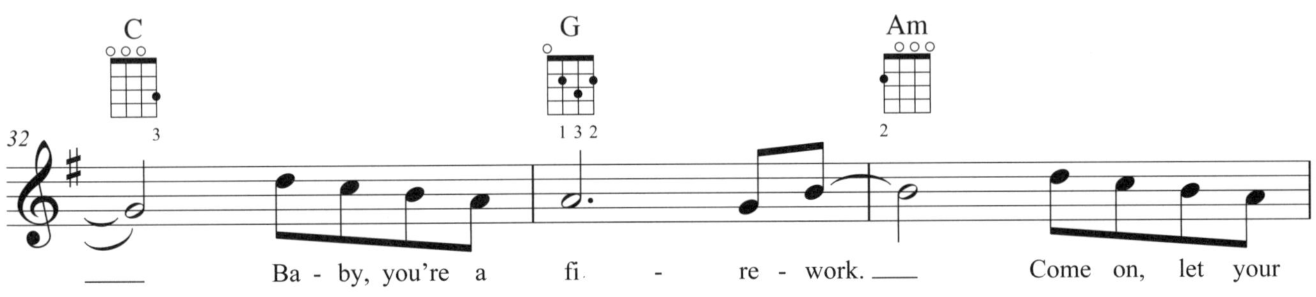
C
G
Am
3
1 3 2
2
32
Ba - by, you're a fi - re - work. Come on, let your

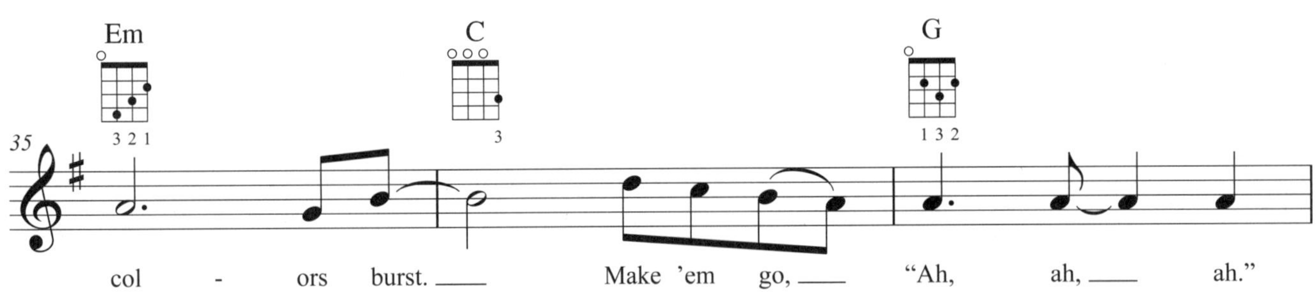
Em
C
G
3 2 1
3
1 3 2
35
col - ors burst. Make 'em go, "Ah, ah, ah."

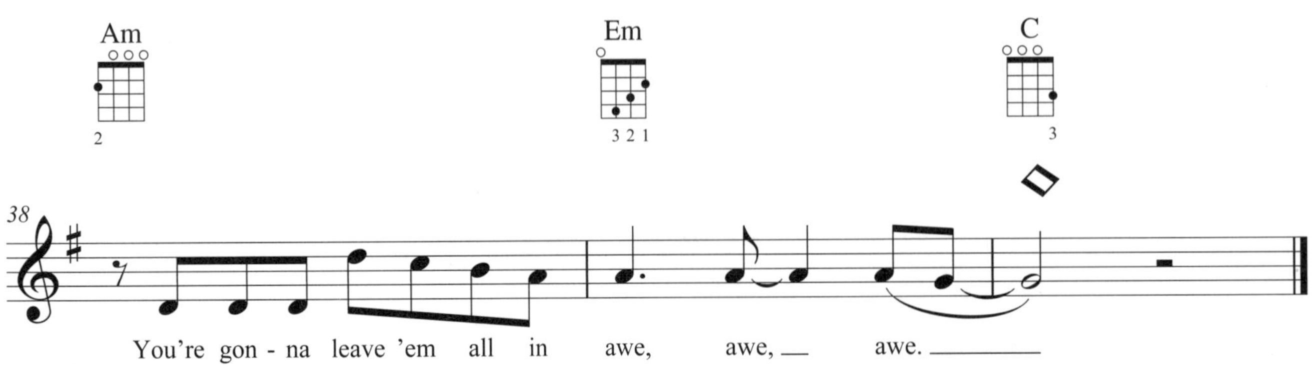
Am
Em
C
2
3 2 1
3
38
You're gon - na leave 'em all in awe, awe, awe.

We'll now try both Em and D in a song. But first, let's practice a new strum, which we'll call Strum Pattern 4. Again, watch the strum directions closely!

Exercise 8: Strum Pattern 4

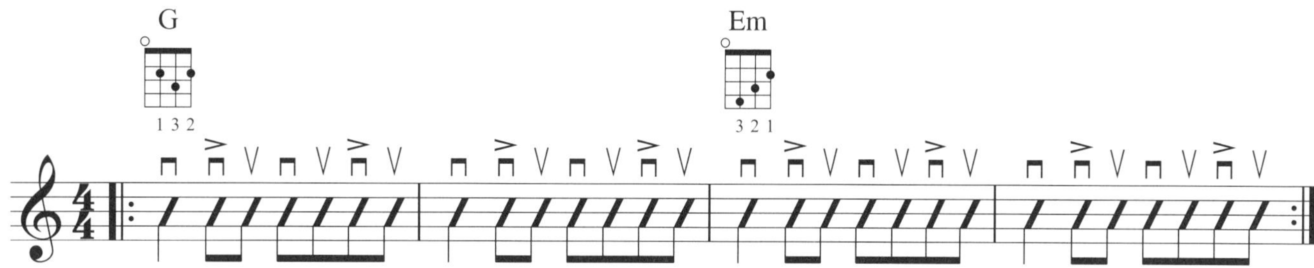

Exercise 9

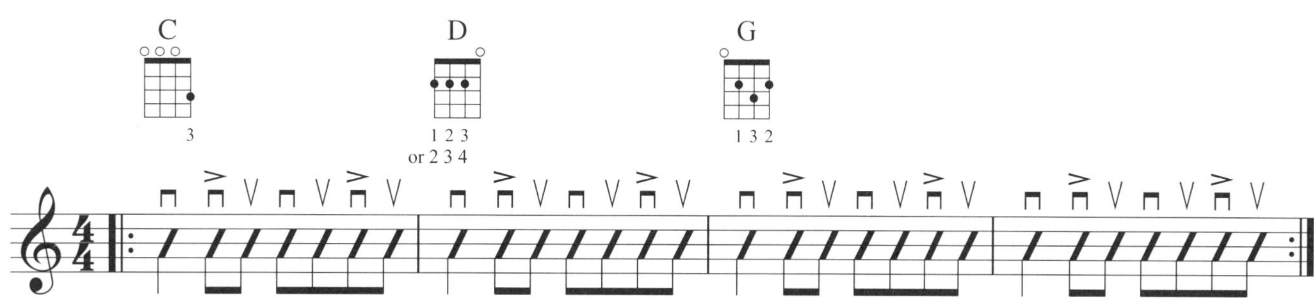

Once you have Strum Pattern 4 down, it's time for "Brave" by Sara Bareilles.

ROUTING DIRECTIONS AND RESTS

In "Brave," you'll see some *routing directions* that you haven't seen yet. These are used as another kind of shorthand (sort of like first and second endings) that saves paper.

- **D.S. al Coda**: This basically means "from the sign to the coda." When you reach this direction, go back to the 𝄋 symbol and play until you see "To Coda ⊕."
- **To Coda**: After starting from the sign, when you reach "To Coda," you jump straight to the Coda (indicated by the ⊕ symbol), which is normally near the end of the song, and continue to the end.

You'll also see a few *rests*. A rest tells you to be quiet for a period of time. Just as there are different rhythms for notes, there are different rhythms for rests:

𝄽 = *quarter rest* (one beat of silence)

𝄼 = *half rest* (two beats of silence)

𝄻 = *whole rest* (four beats of silence)

BRAVE

Words and Music by Sara Bareilles and Jack Antonoff

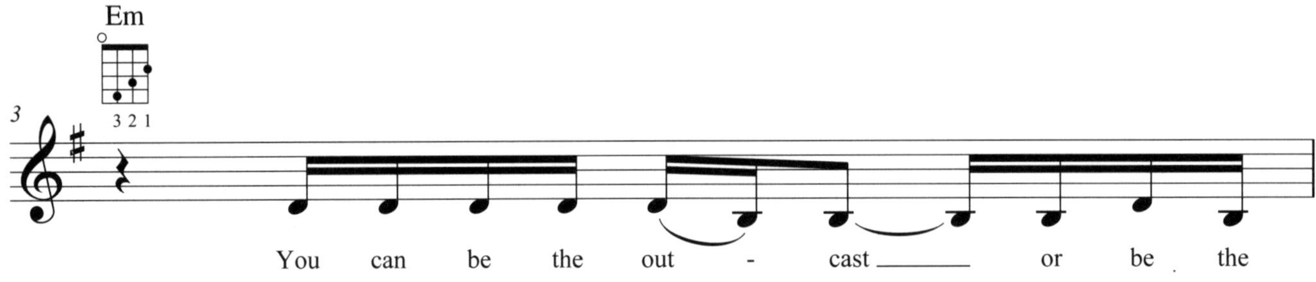

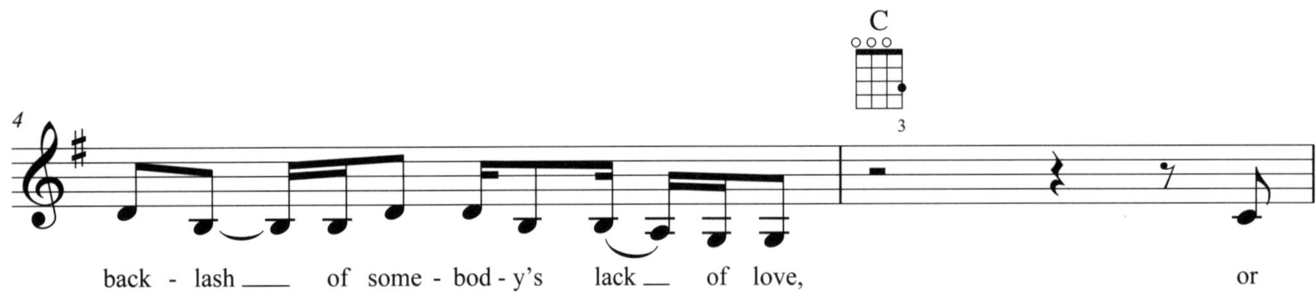

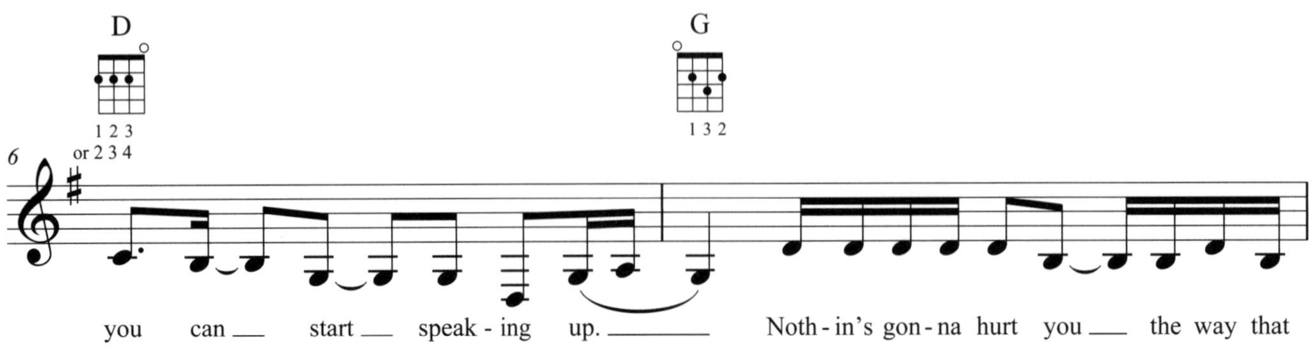

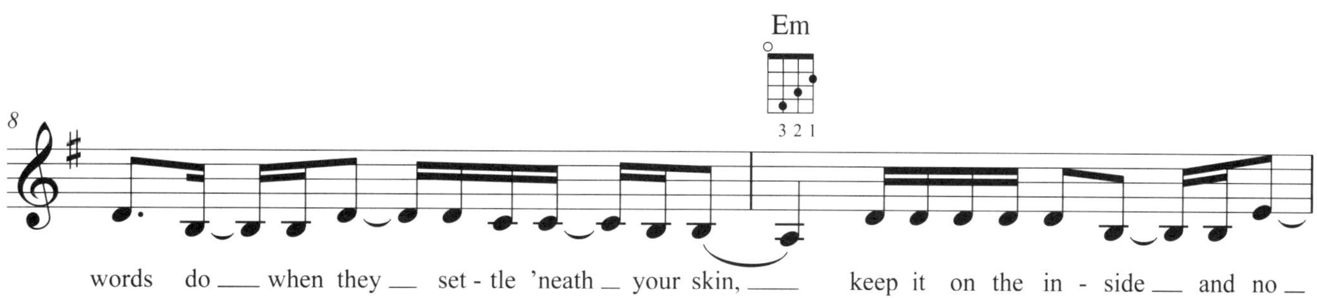
Em
3 2 1
8
words do when they set - tle 'neath your skin, keep it on the in - side and no

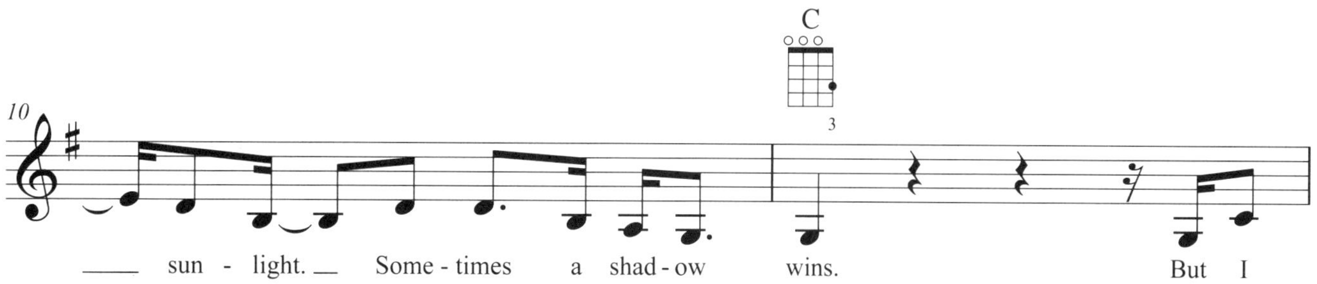
C
3
10
sun - light. Some - times a shad - ow wins. But I

Chorus
D
1 2 3
or 2 3 4
G
1 3 2
12
won - der what would hap - pen if you say what you wan - na say
Say what you wan - na say

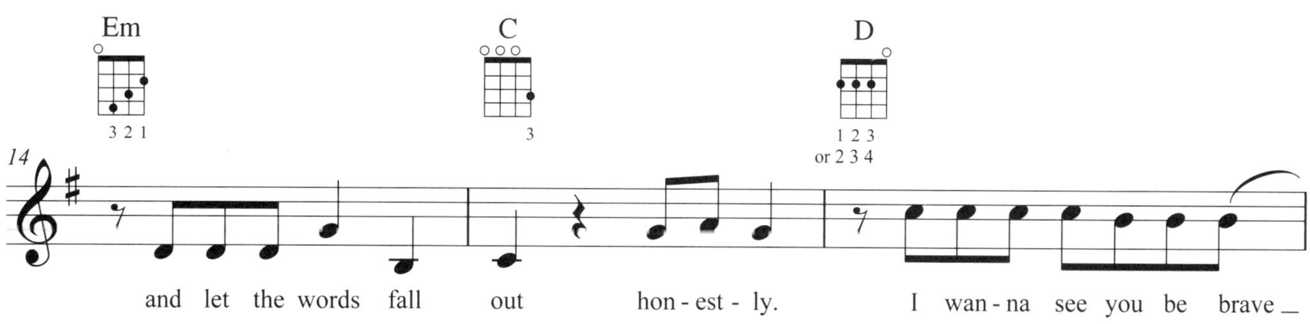
Em
3 2 1
C
3
D
1 2 3
or 2 3 4
14
and let the words fall out hon - est - ly. I wan - na see you be brave

G
1 3 2
Em
3 2 1
17
with what you wan - na say and let the words fall

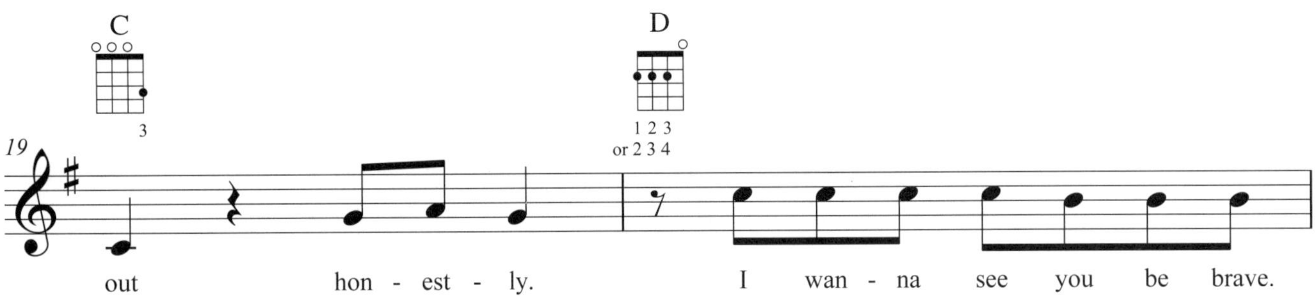
C
3
D
1 2 3
or 2 3 4
19
out hon - est - ly. I wan - na see you be brave.
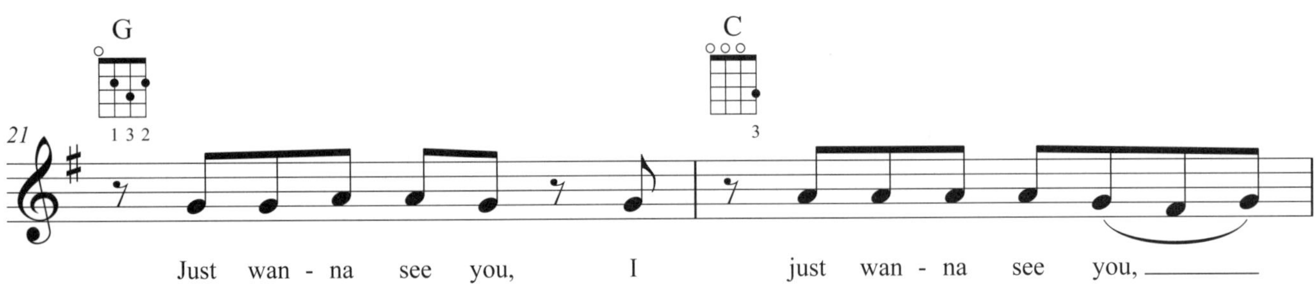
G
1 3 2
C
3
21
Just wan - na see you, I just wan - na see you,
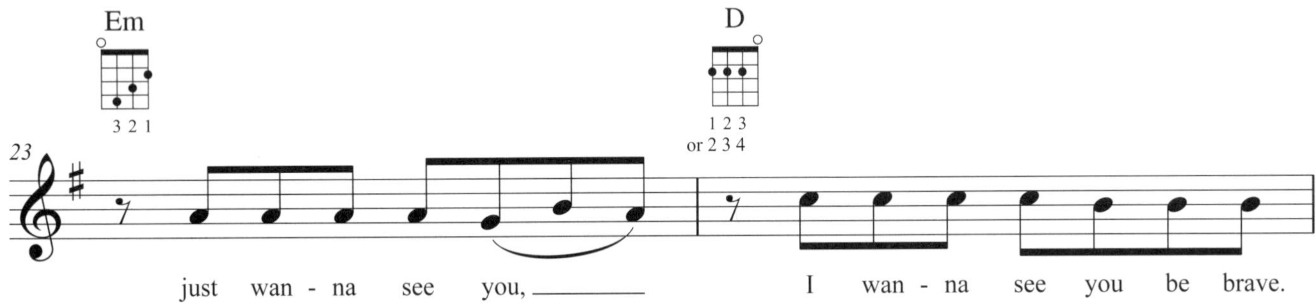
Em
3 2 1
D
1 2 3
or 2 3 4
23
just wan - na see you, I wan - na see you be brave.
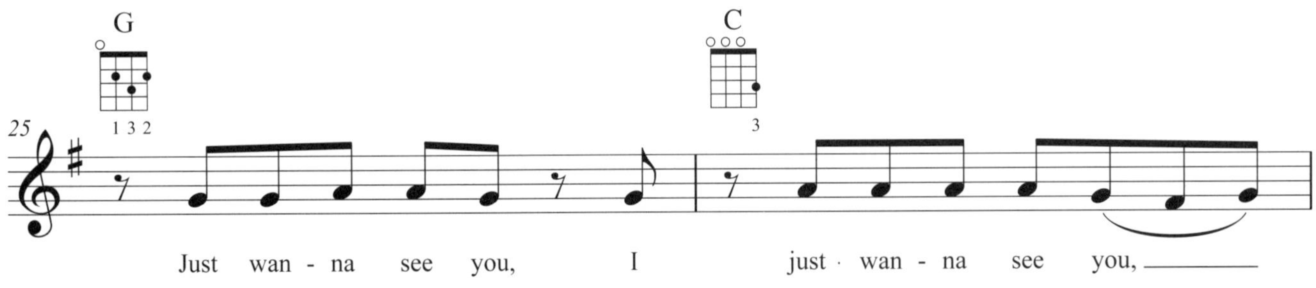
G
1 3 2
C
3
25
Just wan - na see you, I just wan - na see you,
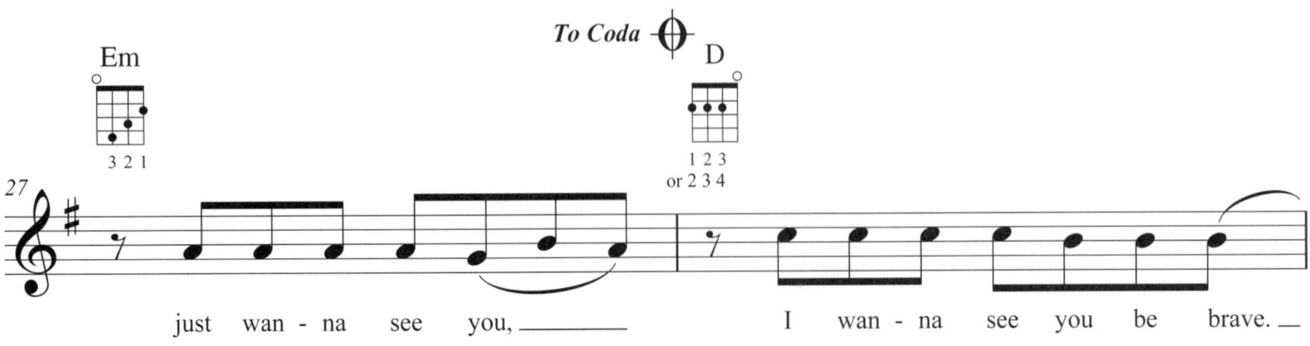
To Coda
Em
3 2 1
D
1 2 3
or 2 3 4
27
just wan - na see you, I wan - na see you be brave.

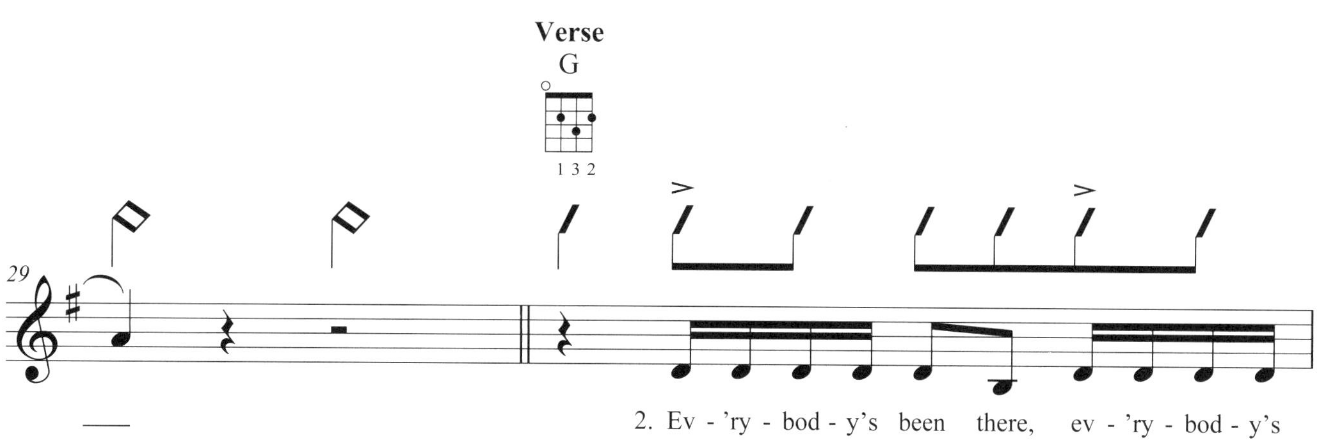
Verse
G
1 3 2
29
2. Ev - 'ry - bod - y's been there, ev - 'ry - bod - y's

Em
3 2 1
31
sim.
been stared down by the en - e - my. Fall - en for the fear and done some dis - ap -

C
3
33
pear - in', bow down to the might - y. Don't run,

D
1 2 3
or 2 3 4
G
1 3 2
35
just stop hold - in' your tongue. May - be there's a way

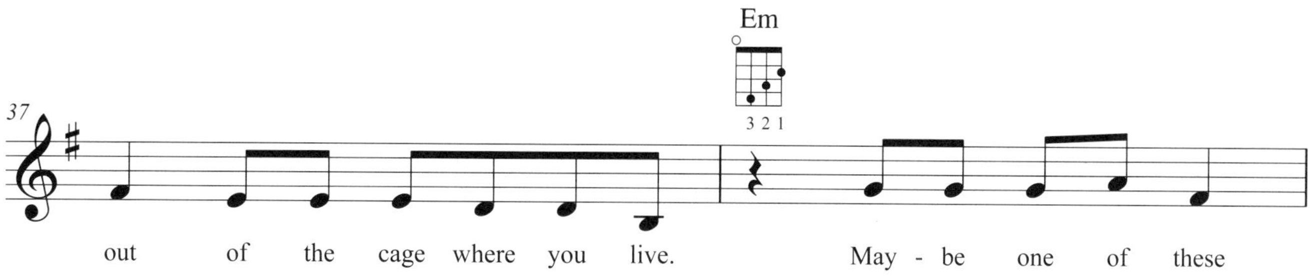
Em
3 2 1
37
out of the cage where you live. May - be one of these

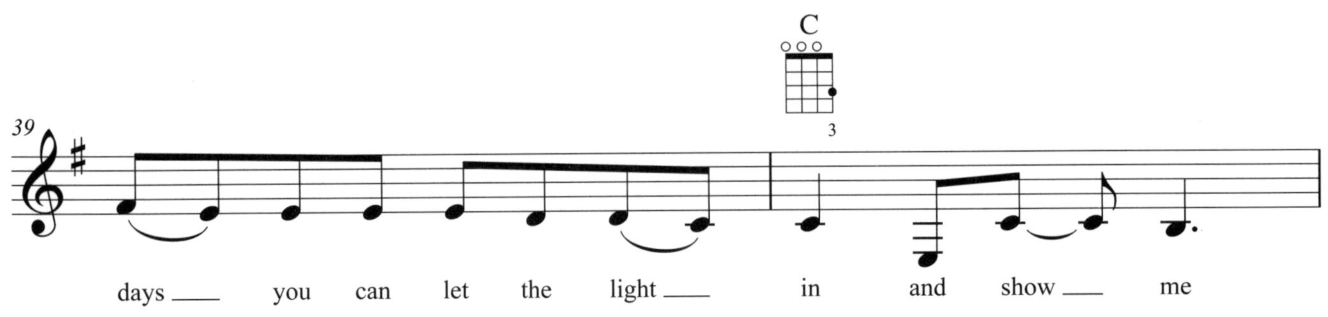

39
C
3
days you can let the light in and show me

Chorus
D
1 2 3
or 2 3 4
G
1 3 2
41
how big your brave is. Say what you wan - na say

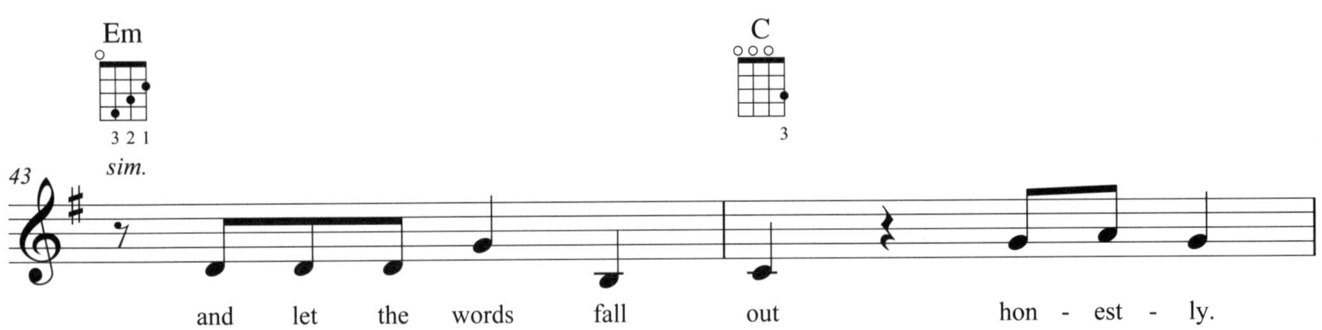

Em
3 2 1
C
3
43
sim.
and let the words fall out hon - est - ly.

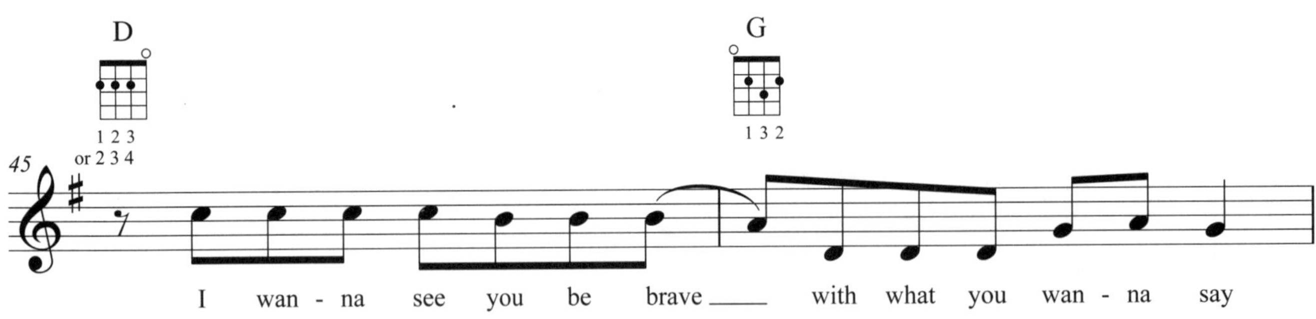

D
1 2 3
or 2 3 4
G
1 3 2
45
I wan - na see you be brave with what you wan - na say

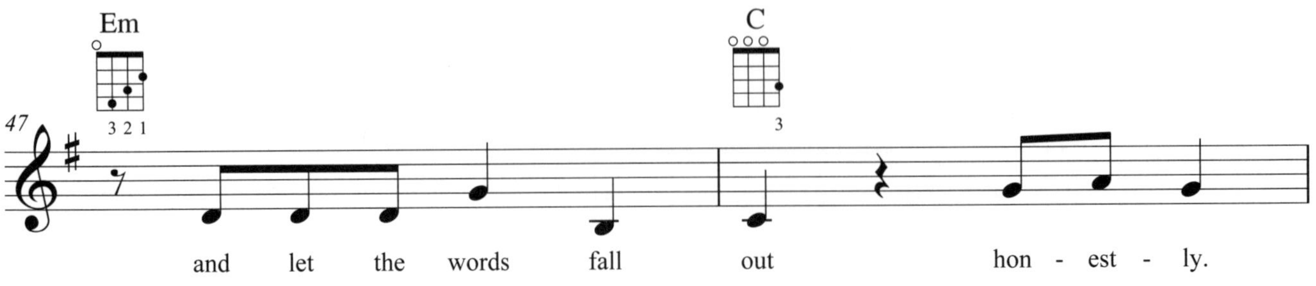

Em
3 2 1
C
3
47
and let the words fall out hon - est - ly.

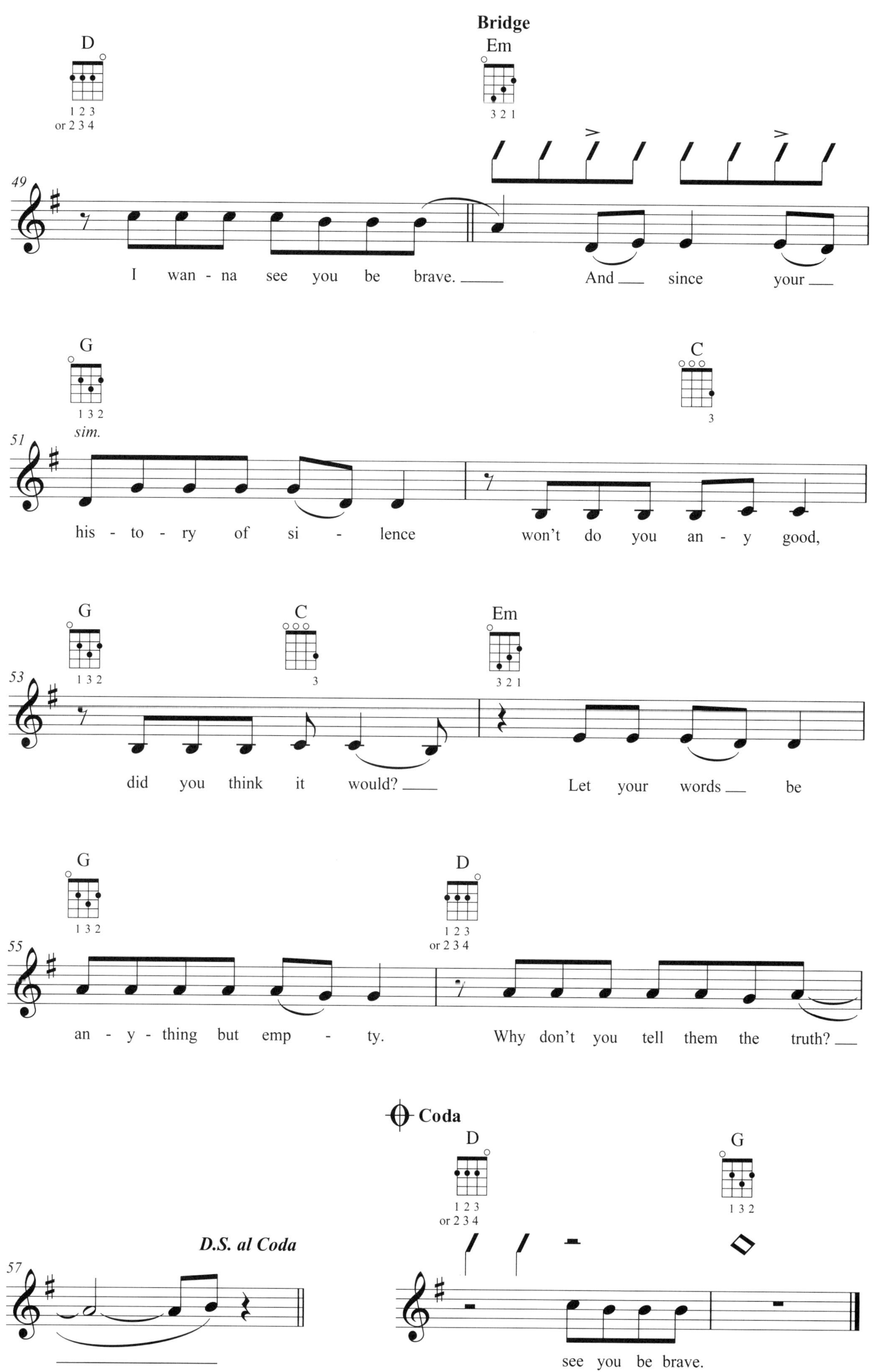

Bridge
D
Em
I wan - na see you be brave.
And since your
G
sim.
C
his - to - ry of si - lence
won't do you an - y good,
G
C
Em
did you think it would?
Let your words be
G
D
an - y - thing but emp - ty.
Why don't you tell them the truth?
D.S. al Coda
Coda
D
G
see you be brave.

3/4 METER

So far, we've been playing in 4/4 time, which means there are four beats in each measure. But there are other *meters* (or time signatures) as well. In 3/4, there are only three beats per measure. So it's just like 4/4, but we count to three in each measure instead of four.

Let's try a simple strum pattern in 3/4 with our F and C chords. We'll call this Strum Pattern 5, and we'll just strum straight quarter notes with an accent on beat 1. Use all downstrums for this.

Exercise 10: Strum Pattern 5

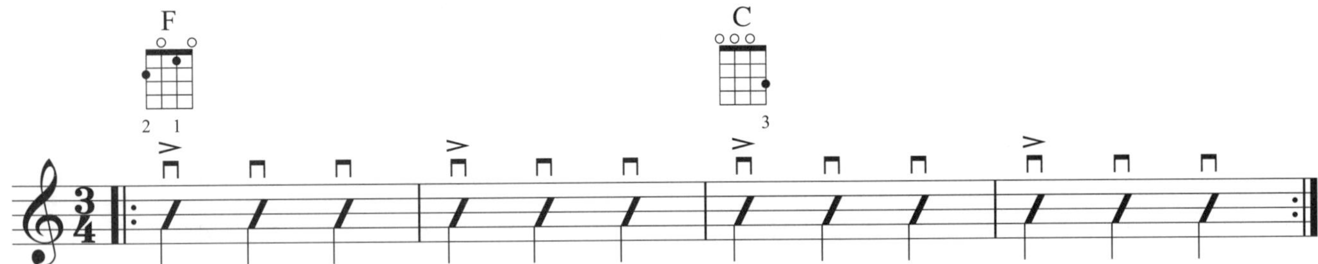

THE WALTZ

3/4 is also known as *waltz meter*, because the waltz is a dance performed to songs in 3/4 time. Some people like to count the waltz by saying "oom pah pah, oom pah pah," with "oom" being beat 1, and "pah pah" being beats 2 and 3. As shown in Strum Pattern 5, there's usually an accent on beat 1 (the "oom").

Dm CHORD

It's time for another minor chord! Dm uses three fingers.

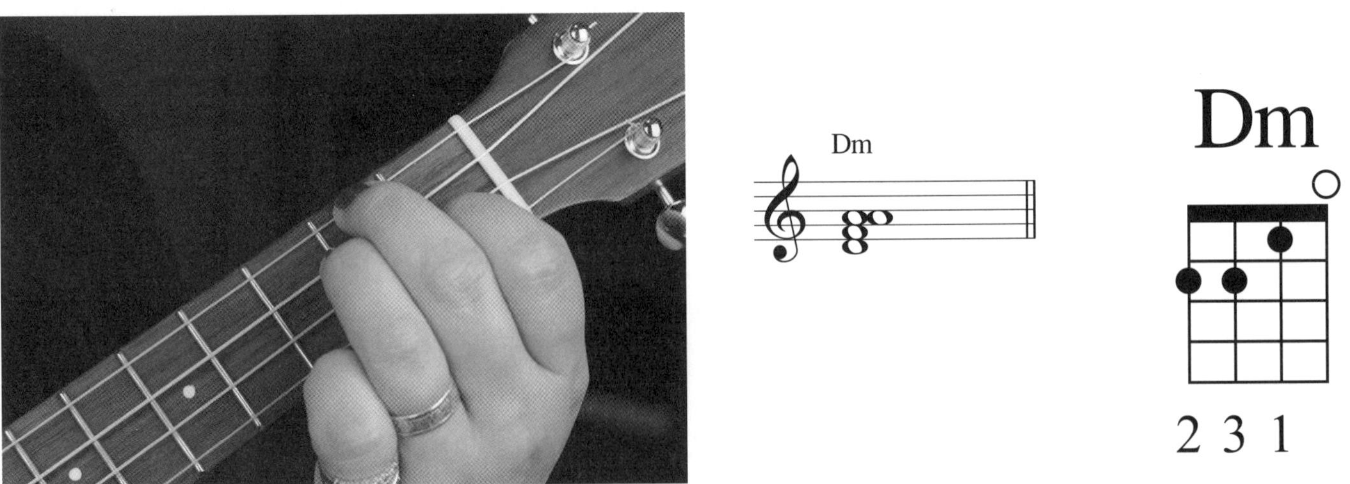

Let's try switching between Dm and C using Strum Pattern 5.

Exercise 11

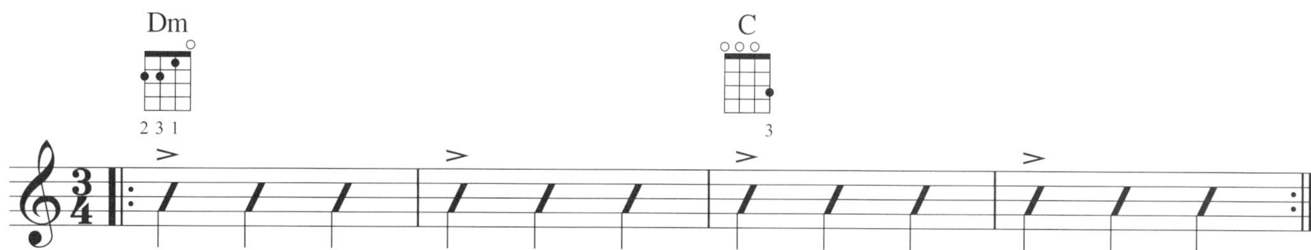

Now let's try Dm and Am.

Exercise 12

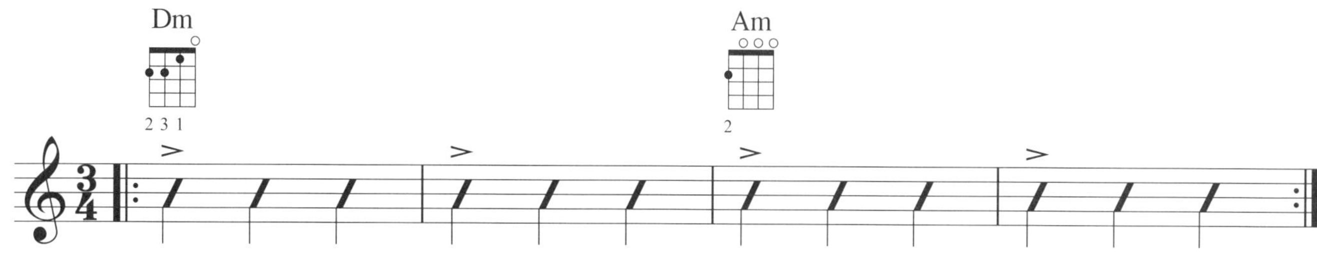

Let's play our first song in 3/4. Christina Perri's "A Thousand Years" uses our new Dm chord and mostly Strum Pattern 5.

HEADS UP!

You'll see two new musical symbols at the very end of "A Thousand Years."

The first is a dotted half note (which also appears at the first ending): 𝅗𝅥. . A *dot* after a note increases the rhythmic value by half. Since a half note is held for two beats, and one is half of two, then a dotted half note is held for three beats (two plus one). Since we're in 3/4 here, a dotted half note takes up a whole measure.

The second new symbol is the *fermata*: 𝄐. This tells you to hold the note (or chord, in this case) for an extended period of time. It's common to see a fermata at the end of a song, because the last chord is often sustained for a long time.

A THOUSAND YEARS

from the Summit Entertainment film THE TWILIGHT SAGA: BREAKING DAWN - PART 1

Words and Music by David Hodges
and Christina Perri

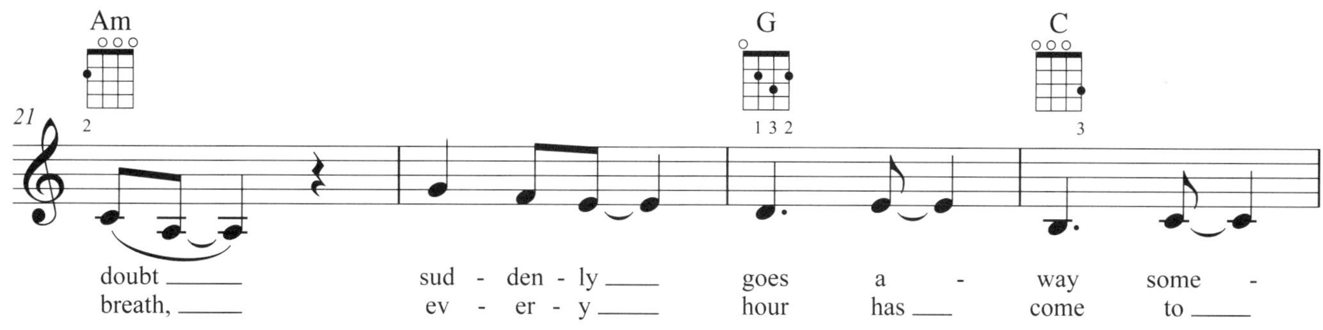
Am
G
C
21
doubt
breath,
sud - den - ly
ev - er - y
goes
hour
a -
has
way
come
some -
to

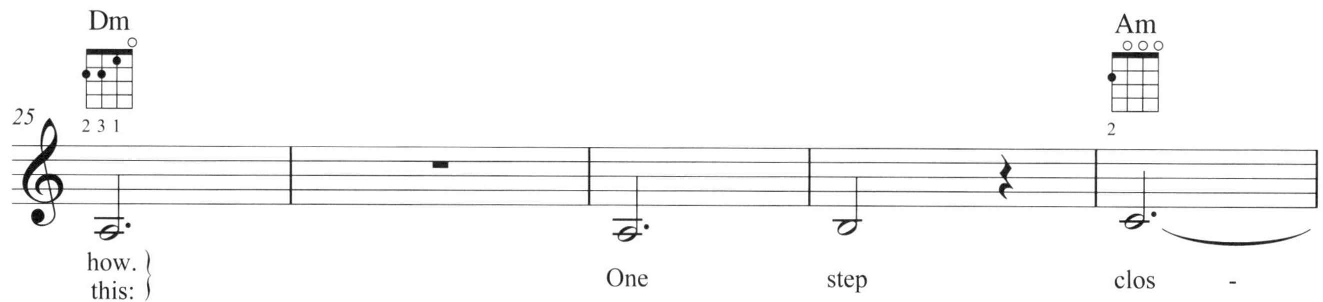
Dm
Am
25
how.
this:
One
step
clos -

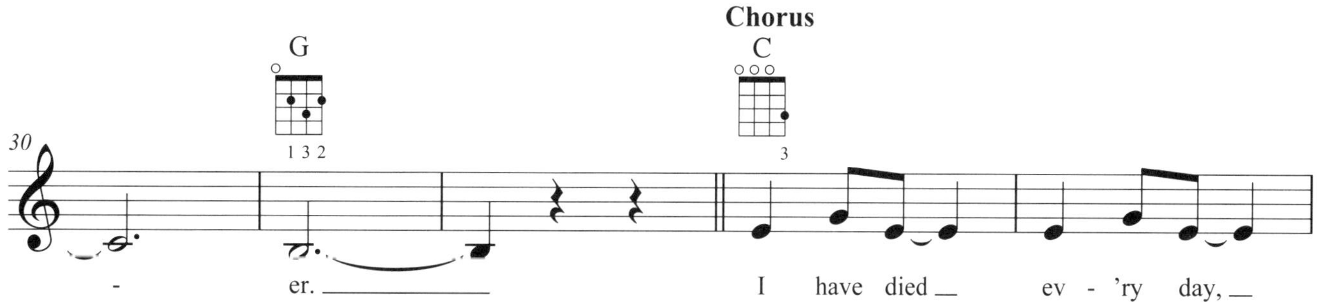
Chorus
G
C
30
- er.
I have died
ev - 'ry day,

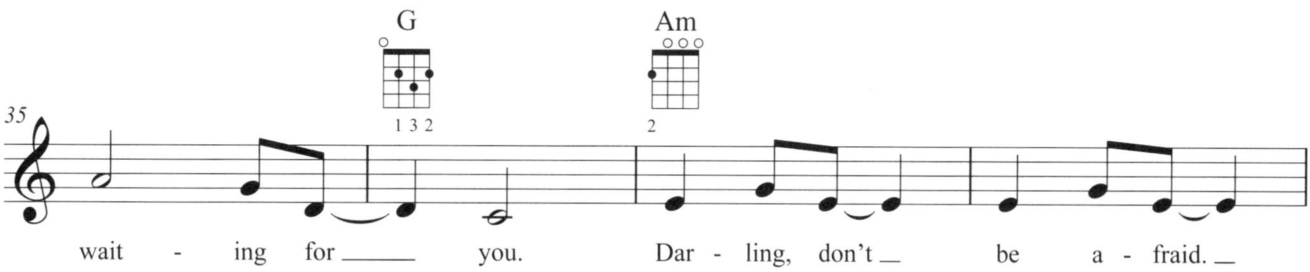
G
Am
35
wait - ing for
you.
Dar - ling, don't
be a - fraid.

G
F
39
I have loved
you for a thou - sand years,
I'll

G
1.
44
love you for a thou - sand more.
2.
G
Chorus
C
sim.
49
more. And all a - long I be - lieved
G
Am
53
I would find you. Time has brought your heart to me;
G
F
57
I have loved you for a thou - sand years, I'll
G
F
62
love you for a thou - sand more.

CHAPTER REVIEW

Here's what we learned in this chapter:

- Three new chords: **Em, D,** and **Dm**.
- **Basic strumming technique.**
- **Accents** are louder notes that make the music more dynamic and interesting.
- **Strum Patterns 1–5.**
- The **backbeat** refers to beats 2 and 4.
- **Eighth notes** get half a beat.
- **Downstrums** and **upstrums**.
- **Shuffle feel** or **swing feel** is the lopsided rhythm in which the first eighth note in each beat is longer than the second.
- Sometimes an **alternate chord fingering** helps move to a different chord more easily.
- Four songs: **"I'm Yours," "Firework," "Brave,"** and **"A Thousand Years."**
- **Early release** is lifting your fretting hand up on the last eighth note in order to reach the new chord in time.
- **Routing directions:** D.S. al Coda (from the sign to the coda).
- A **fermata** is a symbol that tells you to hold a note or chord for a longer time than normal.
- **Quarter rest, half rest,** and **whole rest** are symbols telling you to be silent for one, two, and four beats.
- **3/4 meter (waltz):** Three beats in a measure, and the quarter note gets the beat.
- A **dot** increases a note's rhythmic value by half.

CHAPTER 3: MORE CHORDS AND STRUM PATTERNS

In this chapter, we'll continue adding to our collection of chords and strum patterns. The more chords and strum patterns you know, the more songs you can play!

SYNCOPATION

The word *syncopation* basically means "a stress on the weak beat." For our purposes here, this will mean stressing an upbeat in a pattern with eighth notes. So we'll be stressing one of the "and" counts.

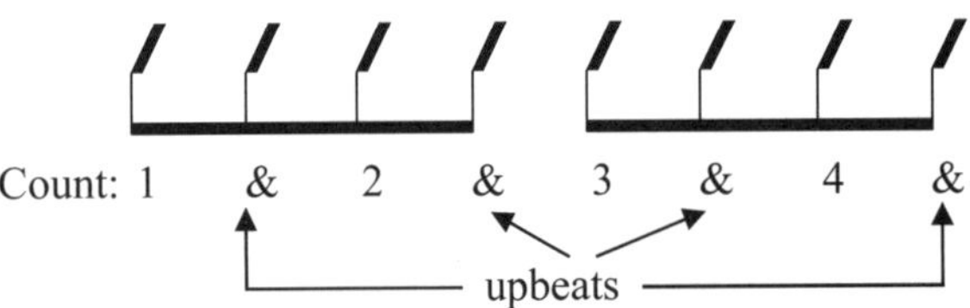

By leaving out a downstrum immediately after an upstrum, we can create a syncopated pattern, because this will naturally put a stress on the upbeat.

Let's look at Strum Pattern 4 again:

Strum Pattern 4

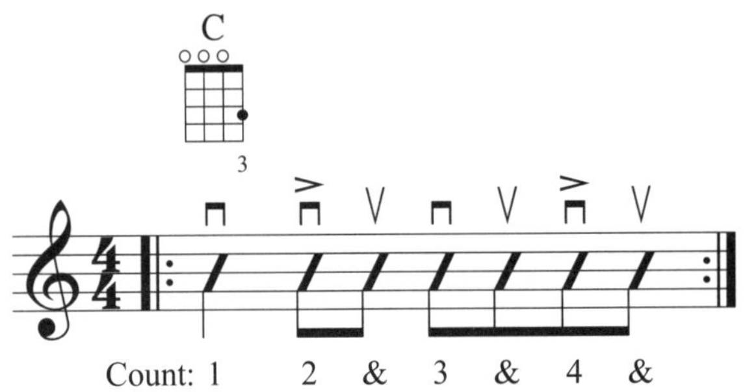

Now, if we leave out the downstrum on beat 3, we'll create a very common strum pattern that's sometimes called the "ukulele strum." We'll label this Strum Pattern 6. The curved line ⌢ is a *tie*, and it connects the rhythmic values of two (or more) of the same notes or chords. In other words, you strum the first chord and it lasts for the duration of both chords combined.

HEADS UP!

Pay *very close* attention to the strum directions here! Notice that both the count on beat 3 and the downstrum above beat 3 are in parentheses. This means that you're strumming down here, but you're *missing the strings on purpose*! This sets you up for the following upstrum.

Exercise 1: Strum Pattern 6

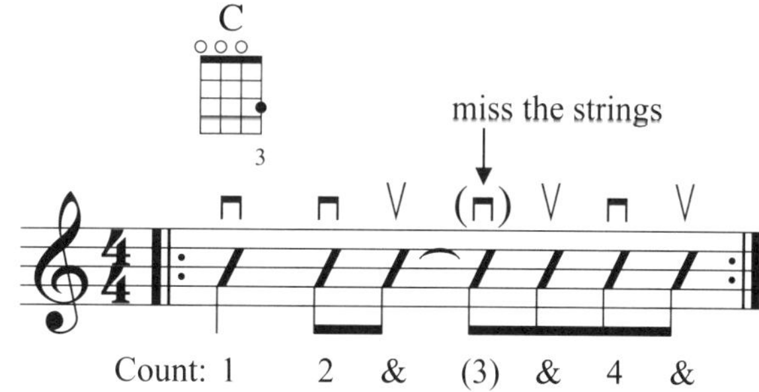

Let's try playing this pattern with a shuffle rhythm now and switch between C and F chords.

Exercise 2

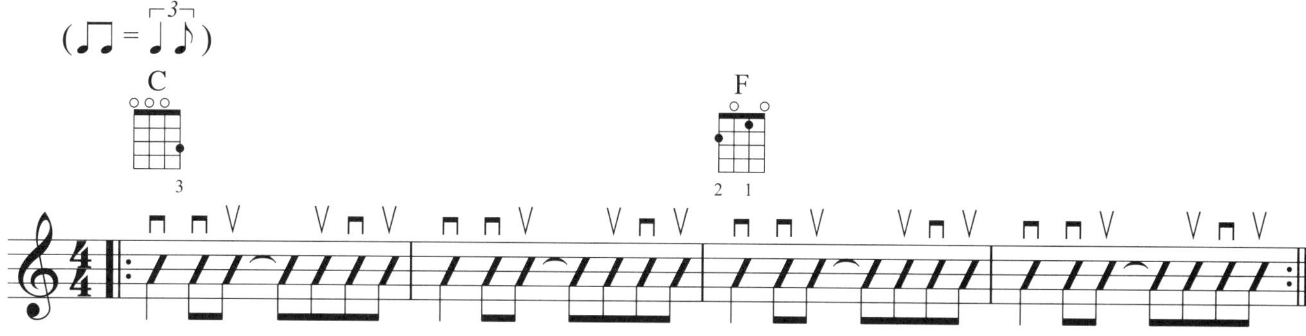

Practice this strum pattern until it's second nature, because you'll come across it a lot! Next up is an example of it with Grace VanderWaal's "I Don't Know My Name." Note that Strum Pattern 3 is also used.

HEADS UP!

The next song contains a new routing direction, *D.C. al Coda*. This is very similar to the D.S. al Coda that you encountered earlier and basically means, "from the top to the coda." When you reach this direction, go back to the beginning of the song, play until you see "To Coda," and then skip ahead to the Coda section near the end of the song.

I DON'T KNOW MY NAME

Words and Music by Grace VanderWaal

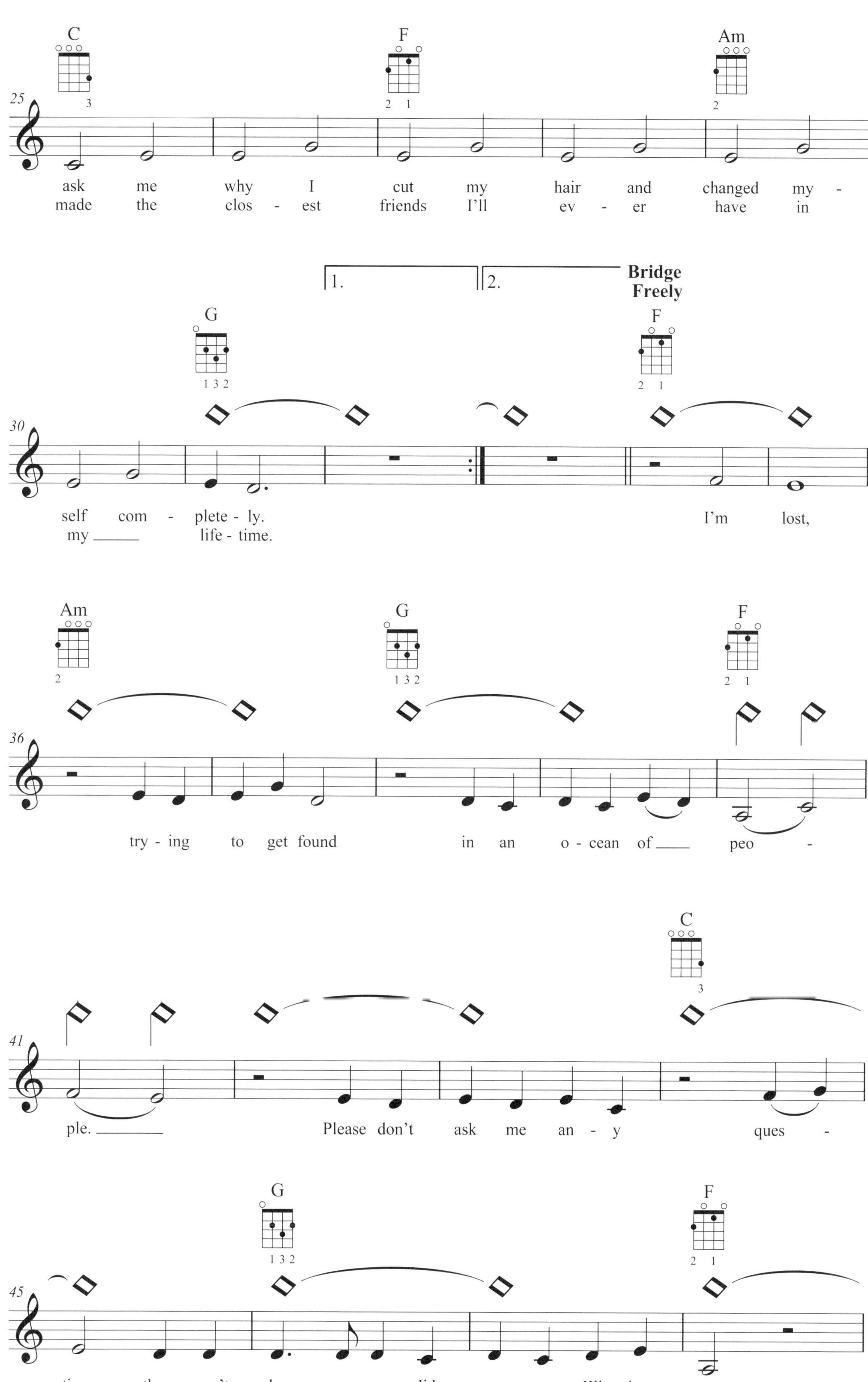

C
F
Am
3
2 1
2
25
ask me why I cut my hair and changed my -
made the clos - est friends I'll ev - er have in
1.
2.
Bridge
Freely
G
F
1 3 2
2 1
30
self com - plete - ly.
my ___ life - time.
I'm lost,
Am
G
F
2
1 3 2
2 1
36
try - ing to get found in an o - cean of ___ peo -
C
3
41
ple. ___ Please don't ask me an - y ques -
G
F
1 3 2
2 1
45
tions; there won't be a va - lid ans - wer. I'll just say

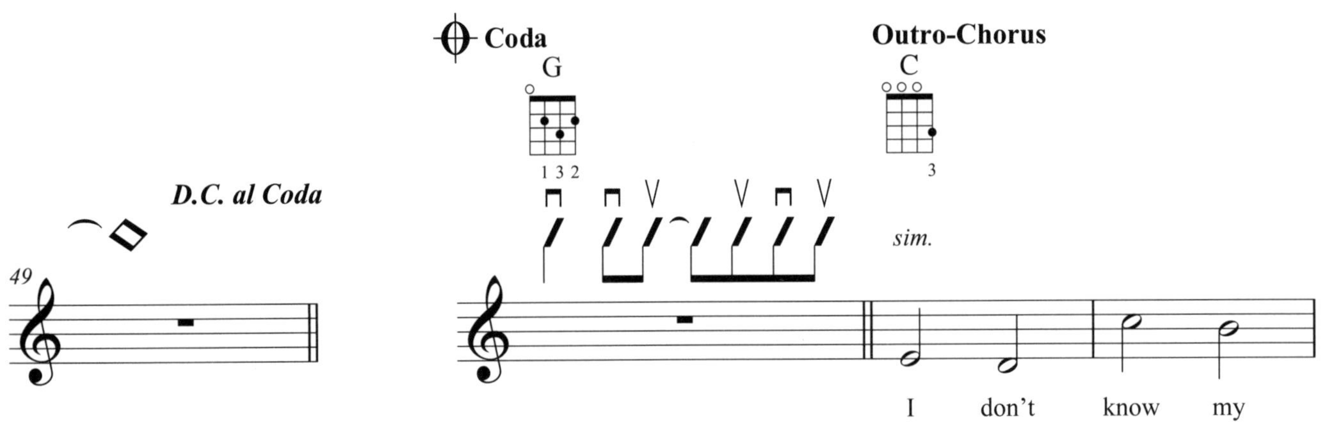
D.C. al Coda
Coda
Outro-Chorus
G
C
sim.
I don't know my
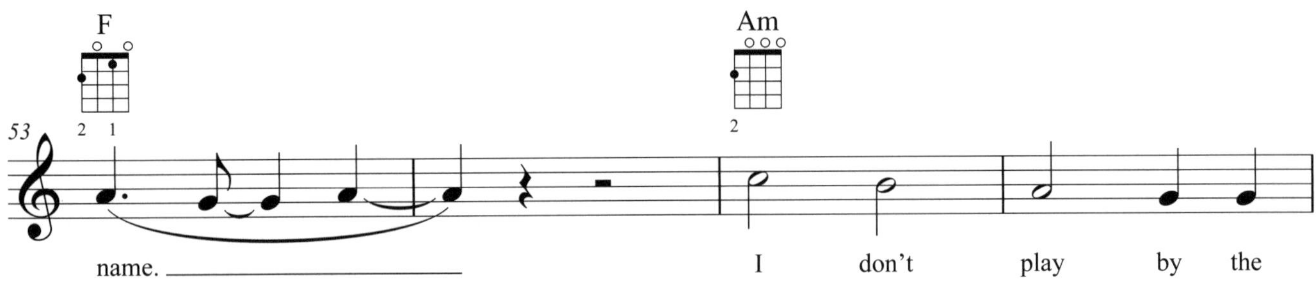
F
Am
name.
I don't play by the

G
C
rules of the game.
So you say
I'm not

F
Am
try - ing,
but I'm
try - ing

G
C
to find my way.

Strum Pattern 6 is also a common pattern in a straight eighth feel (i.e., not swung) as well. For an example of this, we'll play Ed Sheeran's "Photograph" in the key of G with four chords: G, Em, D, and C.

PHOTOGRAPH

Words and Music by Ed Sheeran, Johnny McDaid,
Martin Peter Harrington and Tom Leonard

Pre-Chorus
C
Em
We keep this love in a pho -
C
G
- to - graph.
We made these mem - o - ries for
D
Em
our - selves,
where our eyes
are nev - er clos - ing,
hearts
C
G
are nev - er bro - ken
and time's
for - ev - er fro - zen still.
Chorus
D
G
sim.
So you can keep me in - side the pock - et of your
(D.S.) fit me in - side the neck - lace you got when you were
D
Em
ripped jeans, hold - ing you clos - er till our eyes meet, and
six - teen, next to your heart - beat where I should be.

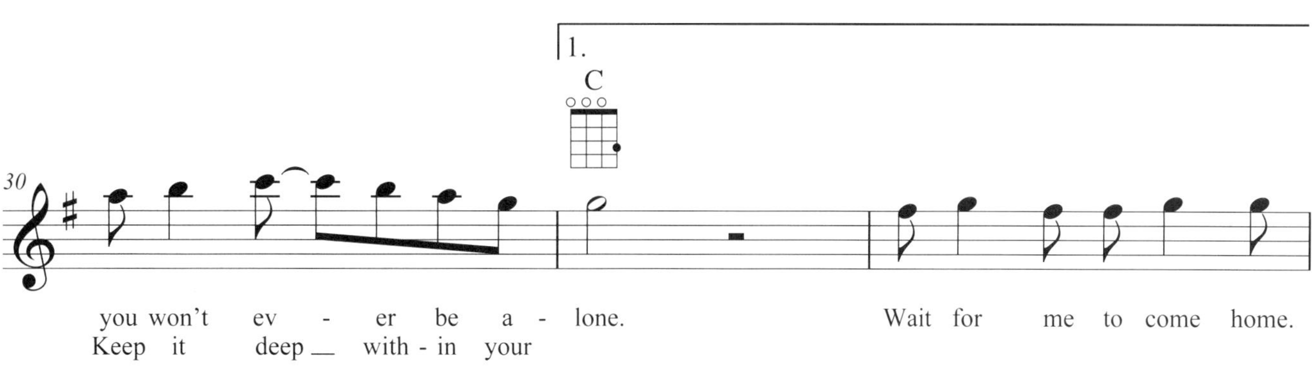
1.
C
30
you won't ev - er be a - lone.
Keep it deep with - in your
Wait for me to come home.

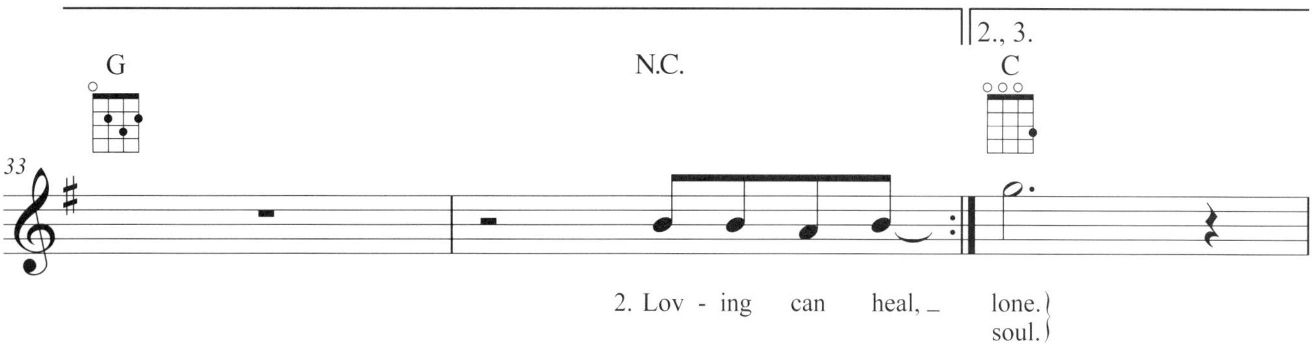
G
N.C.
2., 3.
C
33
2. Lov - ing can heal,
lone.
soul.

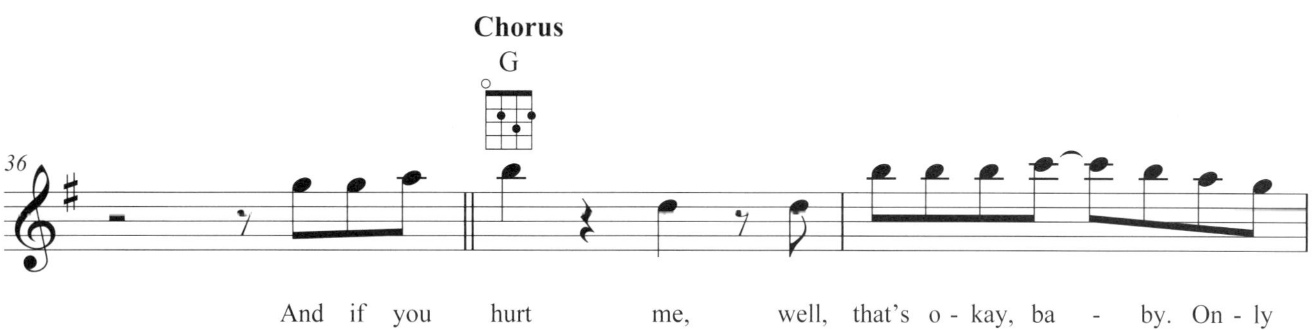
Chorus
G
36
And if you hurt me, well, that's o - kay, ba - by. On - ly

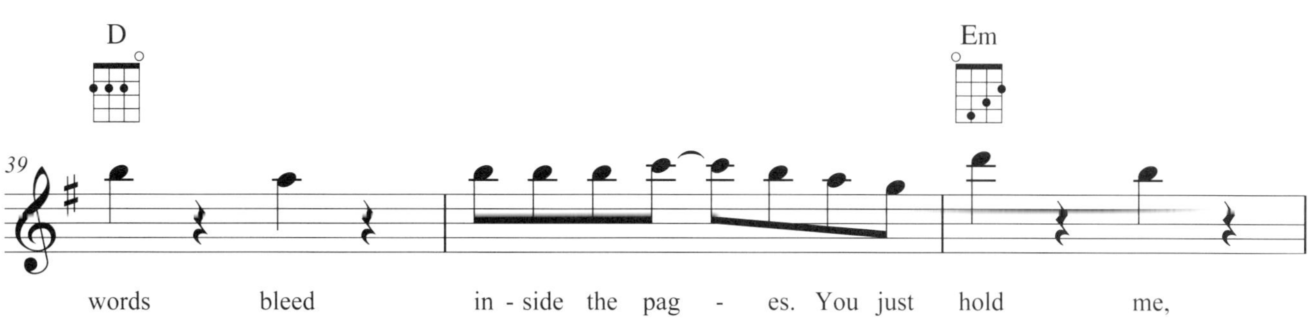
D
Em
39
words bleed in - side the pag - es. You just hold me,

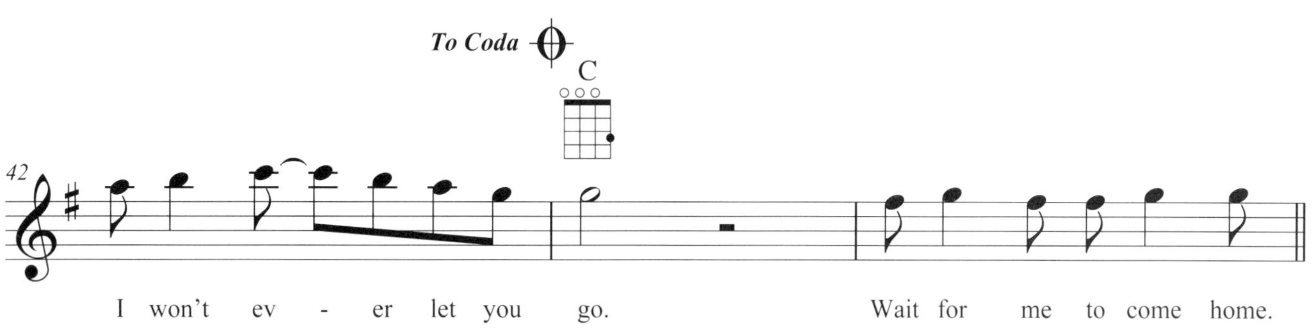
To Coda
C
42
I won't ev - er let you go.
Wait for me to come home.

Bridge
Em
C
Wait for me to come home.

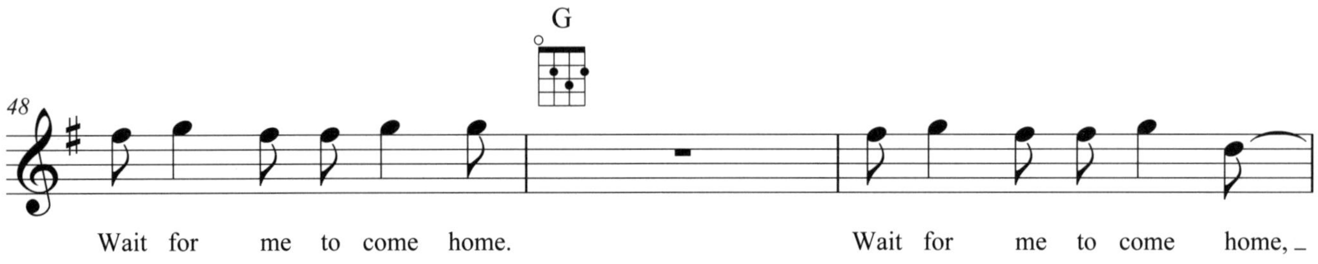
G
Wait for me to come home.
Wait for me to come home, _

D
D.S. al Coda
(take 3rd ending)
Coda
C
ooh.
Oh, you can
go.

Outro-Chorus
G
When I'm a - way,
I will re - mem - ber how you

D
Em
kissed me
un - der the lamp - post back on
Sixth Street,

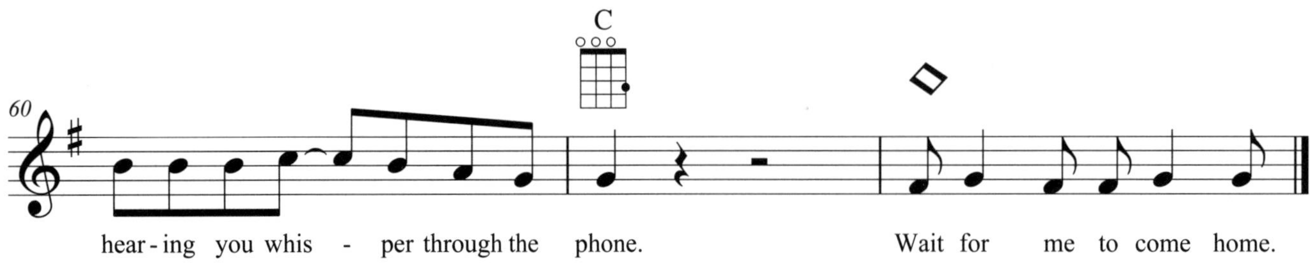
C
hear - ing you whis - per through the phone.
Wait for me to come home.

Csus4 CHORD

Let's learn a couple of new chords now. Csus4, which is short for "C suspended fourth," is neither major nor minor. It's very similar to a C chord, though.

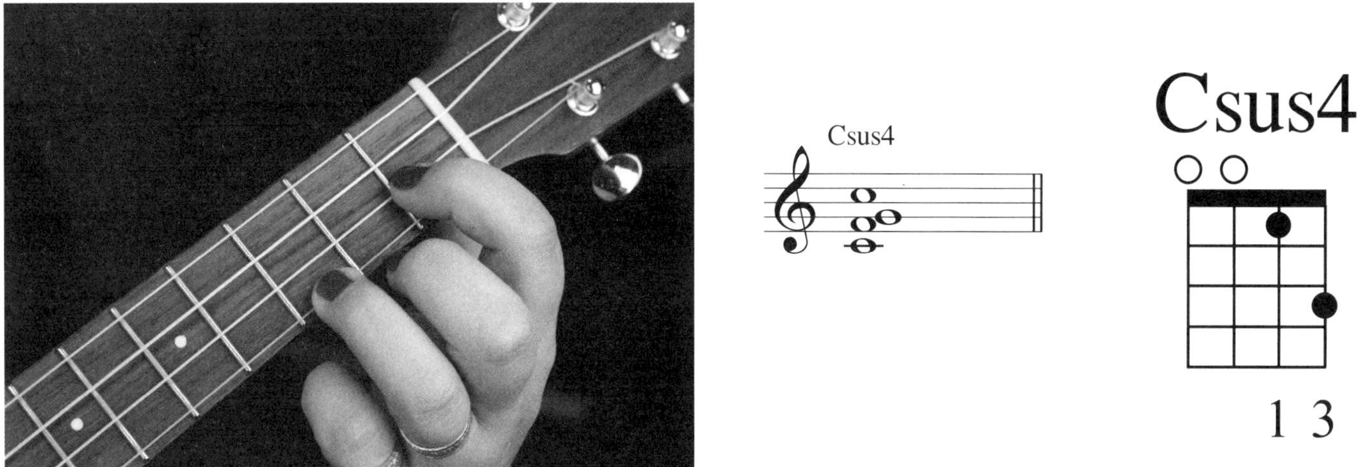

Gsus4 CHORD

And here's Gsus4, which looks a lot like G major.

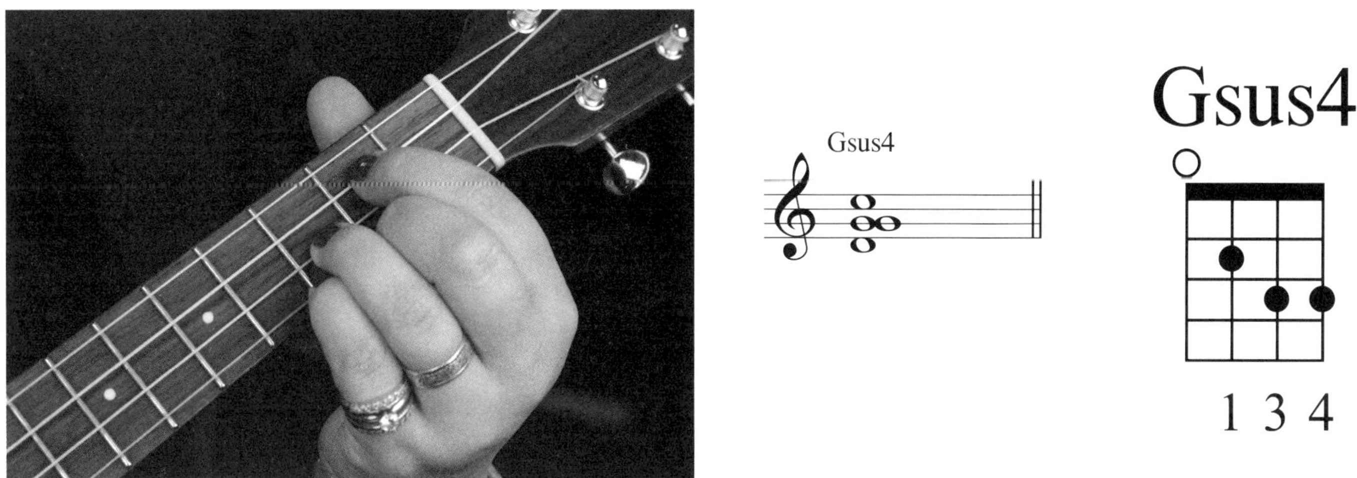

Sus chords are often used to decorate a major or minor chord. Let's try alternating C with Csus4 using Strum Pattern 1. All you have to do is add the first finger for Csus4 and take it off again for C.

Exercise 3

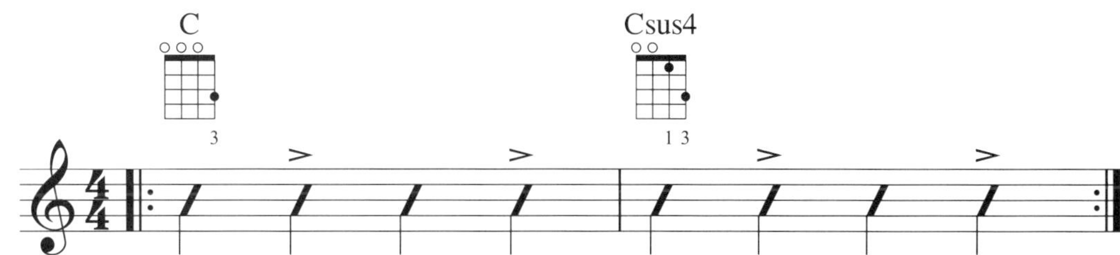

And now let's alternate between G and Gsus4 with Strum Pattern 3. Just add the pinky for Gsus4 and take it off again for G.

Exercise 4

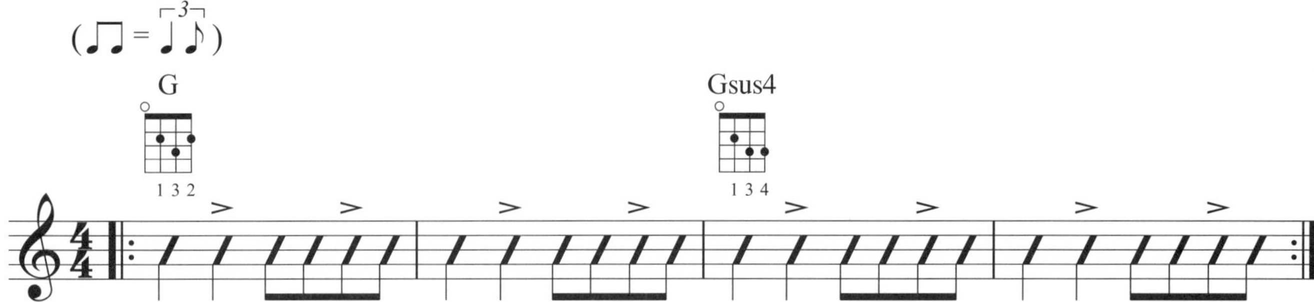

E7 CHORD

It's time for another new chord: E7. Try out both of the fingerings shown to see which feels best.

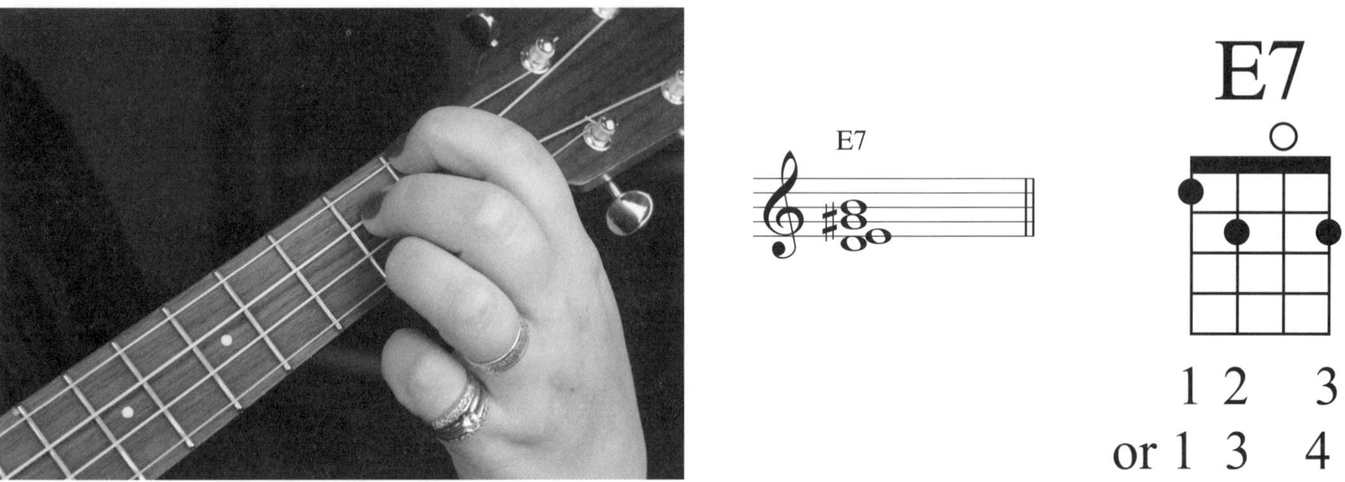

SEVENTH CHORDS

E7 is a *dominant seventh* chord. Seventh chords have four different notes in them. The chords we've been playing so far, *triads*, have only three different notes. Both seventh chords and triads are popular in many different musical styles. Dominant seventh chords sound a bit tense or bluesy.

Let's try using E7 in a progression now. We'll play C–E7–F–C using Strum Pattern 6 (the "ukulele strum").

Exercise 5

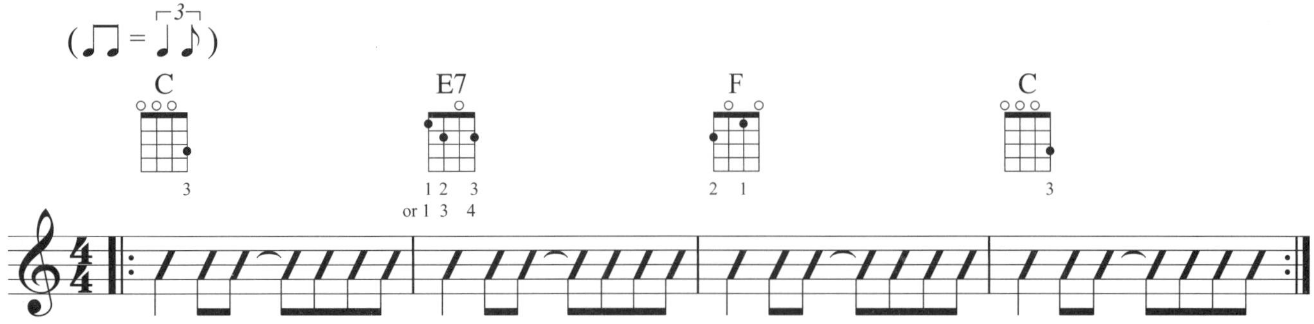

WHICH CHORD FINGERING TO USE? THE "GUIDE FINGER" CONCEPT

You've probably noticed that some chords, like E7, have more than one fingering shown, and other chords that use only one finger, such as C and Am, could be fingered in other ways too. (You could use the second finger for the C chord, for example, or you could use the first finger for Am, etc.) This is partly a matter of personal taste; you may prefer one fingering over another. But sometimes, one fingering will make more sense than the other depending on where you're coming from or going to.

For example, when moving from C to E7, we recommend using the third finger for the C chord and then using the 1–2–3 fingering for E7. Why? Well, your third finger is already on string 1 for the C chord (at fret 3). So all you have to do for E7 is slide it down one fret (to fret 2) and then add the first and second fingers to complete the chord.

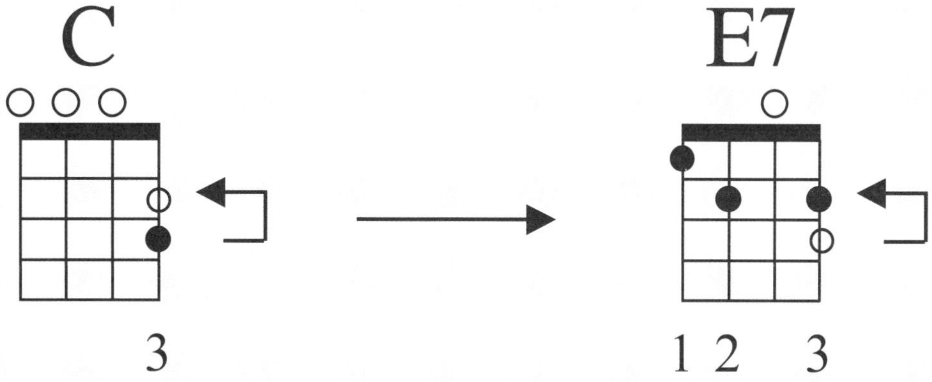

This "guide finger" idea can really make chord transitions easier, so be sure to keep an eye out for any opportunity to use it.

D7 CHORD

D7 is another dominant seventh chord. It's just like D major but with the third string open.

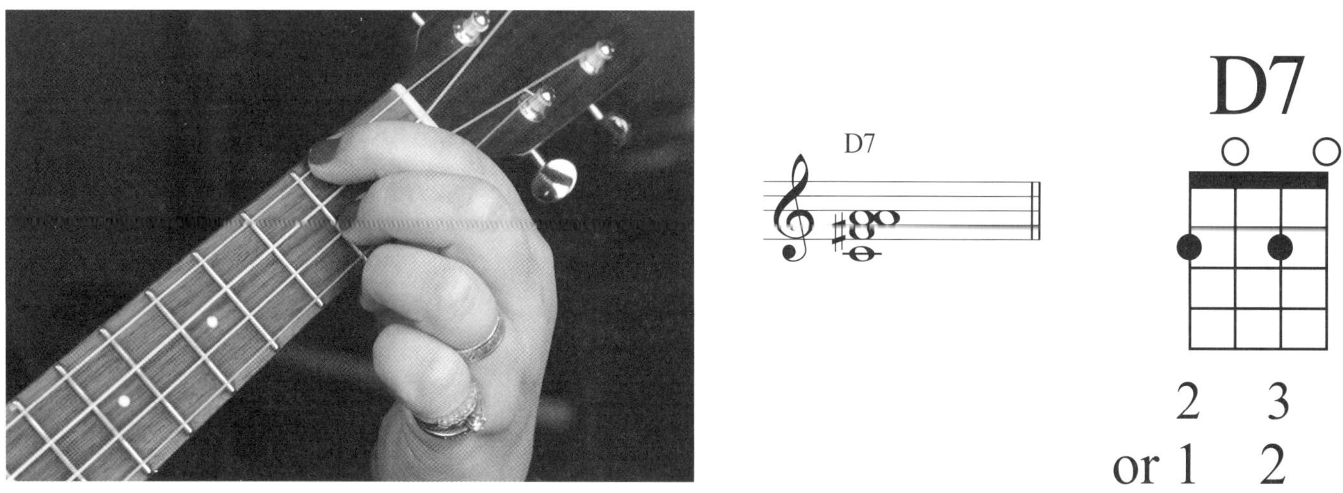

All right, let's try out our new chords—Csus4, Gsus4, E7, and D7—in another song. Ingrid Michaelson's "You and I" uses Strum Pattern 6 with a shuffle feel.

YOU AND I

Words and Music by Ingrid Michaelson

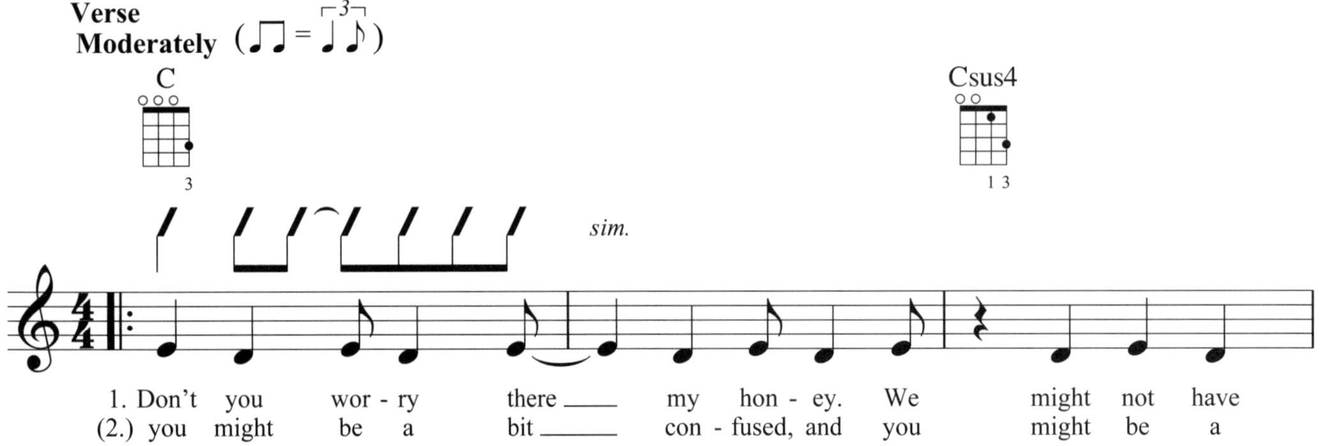

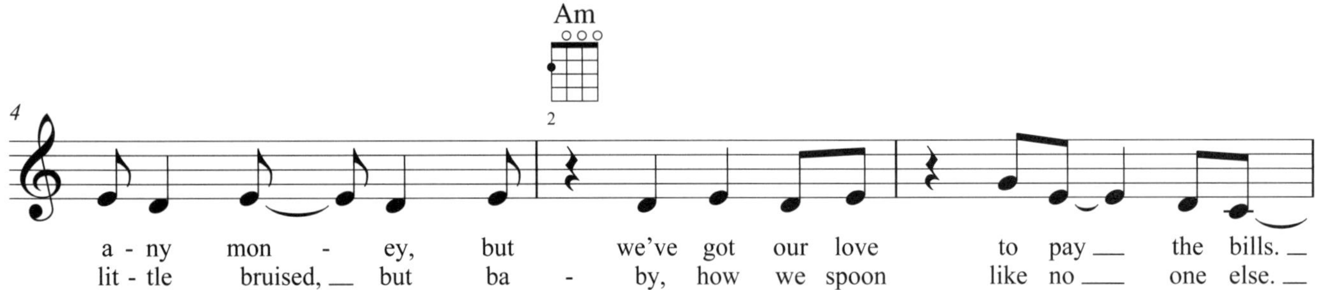

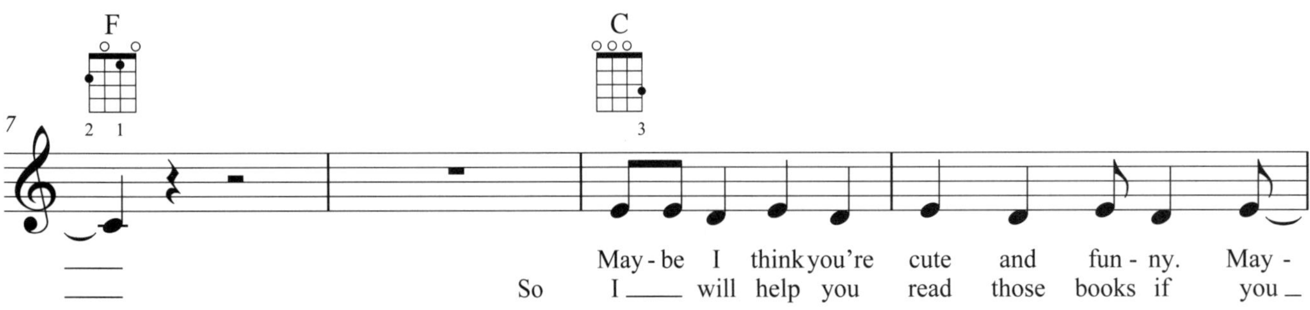

Chorus
F C
know what I mean.
some on the shelf.
Oh, let's get rich and
E7 F C
buy our par - ents homes in the south of France.
Let's get rich
E7 F
and give ev - 'ry - bod - y nice sweat - ers and teach them how to dance.
G C E7
Let's get rich and build a house on a moun - tain, mak - ing
F D7 C
ev - 'ry - bod - y look like ants from way up there.
You and I,
F G C
you and I.
1. 2.
sim.
2. Well,

Gmaj7 CHORD

Gmaj7 is another type of seventh chord: a *major seventh* chord. These chords sound lush and pretty. For Gmaj7, you have two choices:

1. You can *barre*—or lay flat—your first finger across strings 3, 2, and 1 at fret 2 (see photo).
2. You can use a 1–2–3 fingering like the D major chord, but with all your fingers moved up one string (strings 1, 2, and 3 instead of strings 2, 3, and 4).

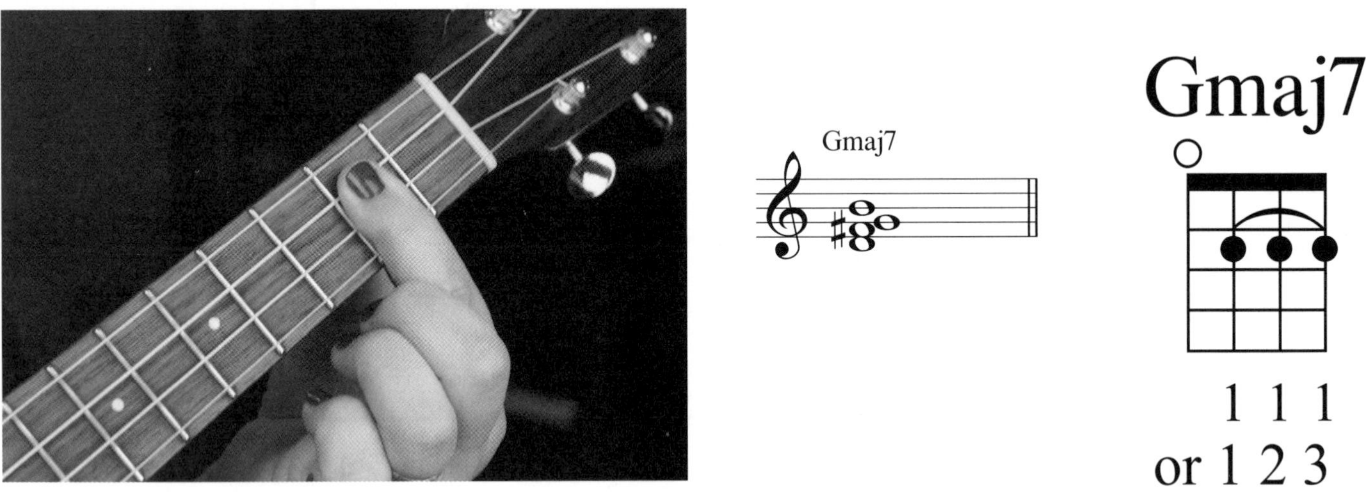

Let's try out these new chords with some exercises. First, let's move from Am to D7 to G. Keep your second finger in the same spot for the Am and D7 chords. Then use your third finger on string 2 as a guide finger when moving from D7 to G.

Exercise 6

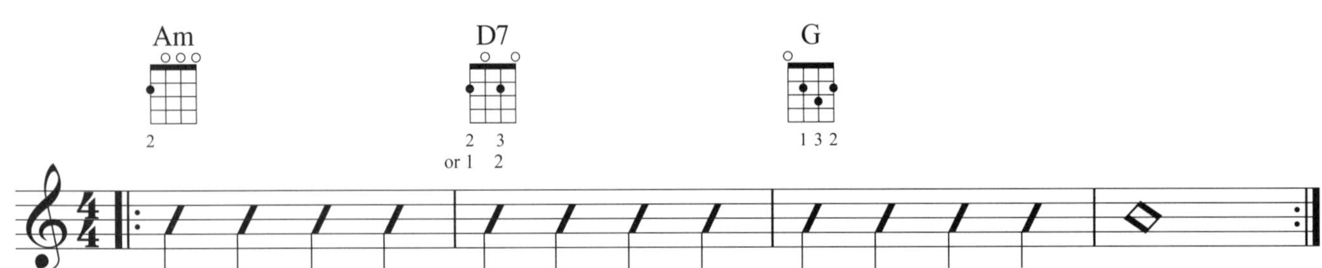

And now we'll use Gmaj7 sandwiched in between G and Em chords.

Exercise 7

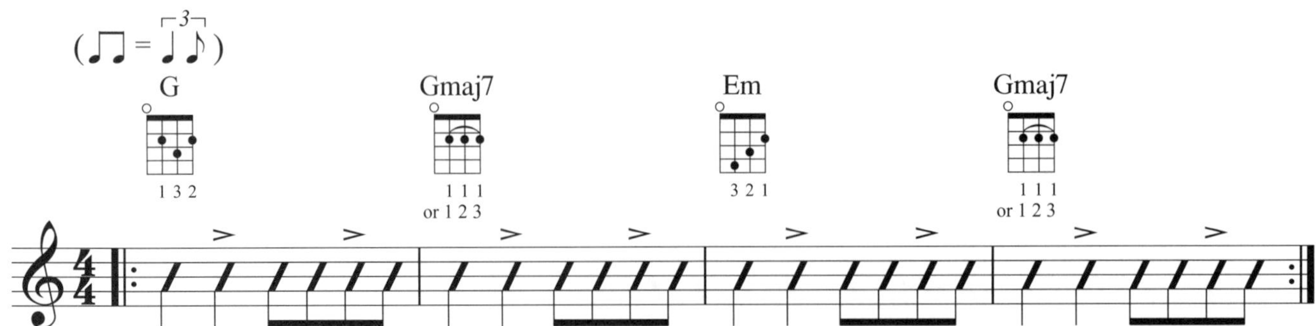

Let's put these new chords to use in "La Vie en Rose." We'll use Strum Pattern 3 with a shuffle feel.

LA VIE EN ROSE (TAKE ME TO YOUR HEART AGAIN)

Original French Lyrics by Edith Piaf
Music by Louiguy
English Lyrics by Mack David

Em
C
11
part, a world where ros - es bloom.
Am
G
13
And when you speak, ang - els sing from a - bove.
Am
D
15
Ev - 'ry - day words seem to turn in - to love
D7
G
17
songs. Give your heart and soul to
Gmaj7
Am
D7
G
sim.
19
me, and life will al - ways be La Vie en rose.

6/8 METER

Besides 4/4 and 3/4 meters, another common time signature is 6/8.

6 = six beats per measure
8 = eighth note gets the beat

So in this meter, we count six eighth notes in each measure, but the first and fourth are naturally accented.

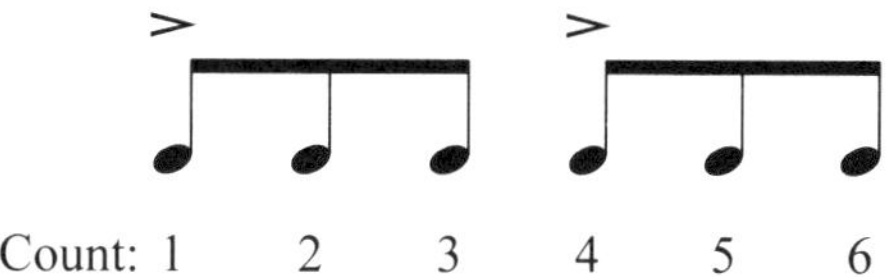

Adding 16th Notes

Just as we can divide one quarter note into two eighth notes, we can further divide one eighth note into two *16th notes.* A 16th note has an extra flag on it when it appears by itself. When two 16th notes appear one after the other, they have two beams instead of one.

So two 16th notes take up the same space as one eighth note. When we count 16th notes in 6/8, we can simply add "and" in between the numbers, like this:

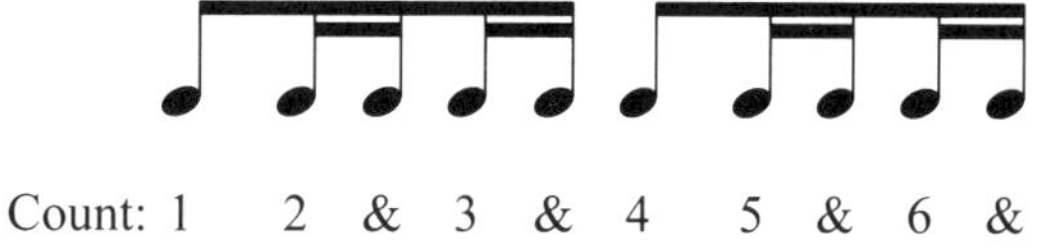

(Notice that beats 1, 2, and 3 are still beamed together, and beats 4, 5, and 6 are still beamed together, even though we've added some 16th notes.)

It turns out the above example is one of the most common 6/8 strumming patterns, so we'll call it Strum Pattern 7. Try it out here on a C chord, and pay attention to the strum directions.

Exercise 8: Strum Pattern 7

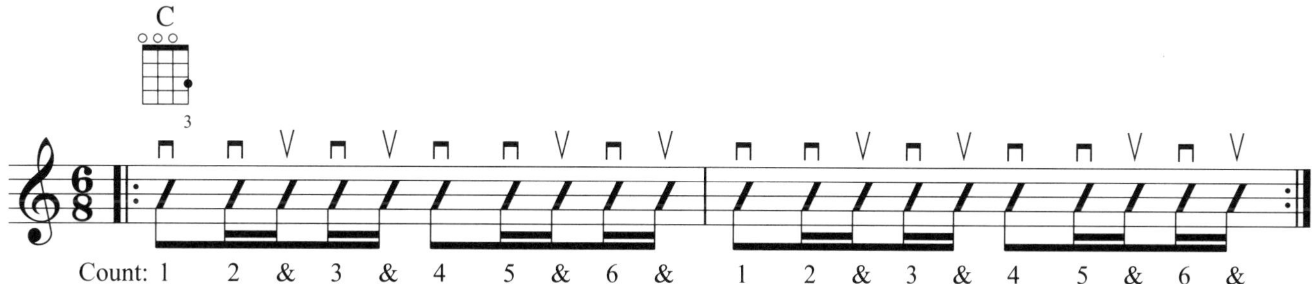

Gm CHORD

Let's add another minor chord so we can play the next song, which is in 6/8. This is a Gm chord.

Let's try using Gm with some other chords. We'll play C–Gm–F–C with dotted quarter notes. Remember that a dot increases a note's value by half. So a dotted quarter note lasts for three eighth notes instead of two.

Exercise 9

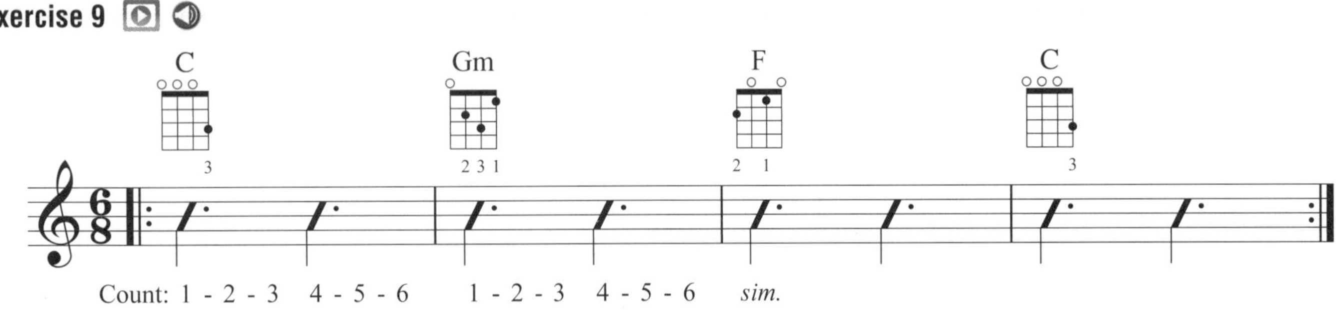

Now we're ready to tackle "The Only Exception" by Paramore. We're using Strum Pattern 7 here with C, Gm, and F chords.

THE ONLY EXCEPTION

Words and Music by Hayley Williams and Josh Farro

Gm
F
watched as he tried to re - as - sem - ble it. And
ways to make it a - lone and keep a straight face. And
C
Gm
my ma - ma swore she would nev - er let her - self for -
I've al - ways lived like this keep - ing a com - f'ta - ble
F
C
get. And that was the day that I prom -
dis - tance. And up un - til now, I had sworn
Gm
- ised I'd nev - er sing of love if it does not ex -
to my - self that I'm con - tent with lone - li - ness,
Chorus
F
C
ist, but, dar - ling, you are the
Gm
F
on - ly ex - cep - tion. You are the on - ly ex - cep - tion.

CHAPTER REVIEW

Here's what we learned in this chapter:

- Six new chords: **Csus4, Gsus4, E7, D7, Gmaj7,** and **Gm.**
- **Syncopation** is stressing a weak beat (or upbeat).
- **Strum Pattern 6**: The "ukulele strum."
- Five songs: **"I Don't Know My Name," "Photograph," "You and I," "La Vie en Rose,"** and **"The Only Exception."**
- **Suspended chords** are neither major nor minor.
- **Seventh chords** have four different notes and are popular in many styles.
- **Dominant seventh chords** sound tense or bluesy. **Major seventh chords** sound lush or pretty.
- The **guide finger concept** is when one finger remains on the same string while changing from one chord to another.
- In **6/8 meter**, there are six beats per measure, and the eighth note gets the beat.
- There are two **16th notes** in one eighth note.
- **Strum Pattern 7**: A common 6/8 strum pattern.

CHAPTER 4: FINGERPICKING

Fingerpicking is another way we can play chords, and it sounds great on the ukulele. In this chapter, we'll learn a few different fingerpicking patterns that can be used to play all kinds of songs.

BASIC TECHNIQUE

To get started, place the thumb of your picking hand on string 4 and your fingers on strings 3, 2, and 1, like this:

Make sure your thumb is in front of your first finger, as shown in the photo. You **don't** want to do this:

This can lead to muscle strain in the thumb and possible injury.

TABLATURE

For this chapter, we're going to introduce a new form of notation called *tablature*, or "tab" for short. A tab staff has four lines—one for each string on the ukulele. String 4 (the G string) is at the bottom, and string 1 (the A string) is at the top.

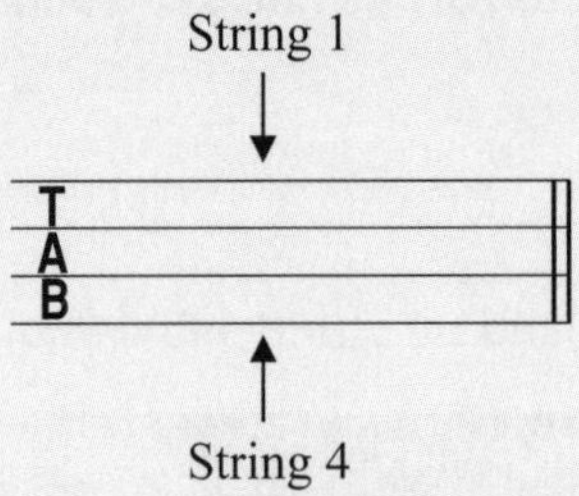

Numbers on the lines tell you which fret to play on that string. A "0" tells you to play the string open (un-fretted). The tab staff is usually paired with a standard notation staff. The notation staff tells you the rhythm and pitches of the notes, and the tab staff tells you exactly where the notes are played on the ukulele fretboard.

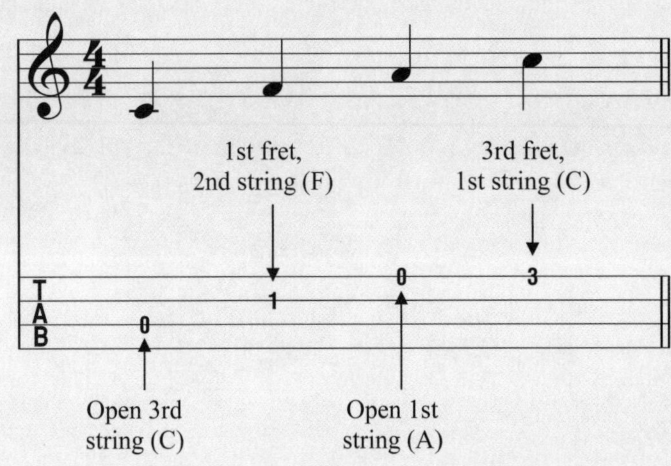

Since we'll be using standard notation as well for the first time here, you can use this fretboard chart as a reference for the notes on the ukulele fretboard. Come back to it whenever you need to find a new note.

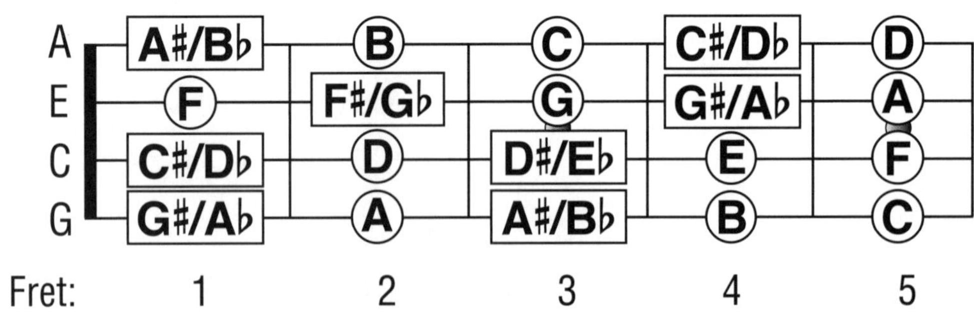

ARPEGGIOS

Once you have the basic fingerpicking position down, try this simple arpeggio exercise with a C chord. An *arpeggio* is the notes of a chord played one at a time instead of all together. The picking-hand fingers are indicated in the music (R.H. = right hand): T = thumb, 1 = first (index) finger, 2 = second (middle) finger, and 3 = third (ring) finger.

Exercise 1

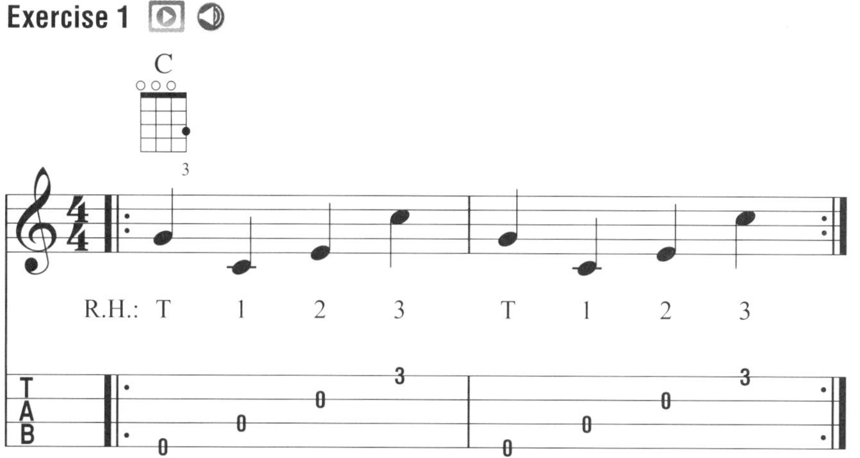

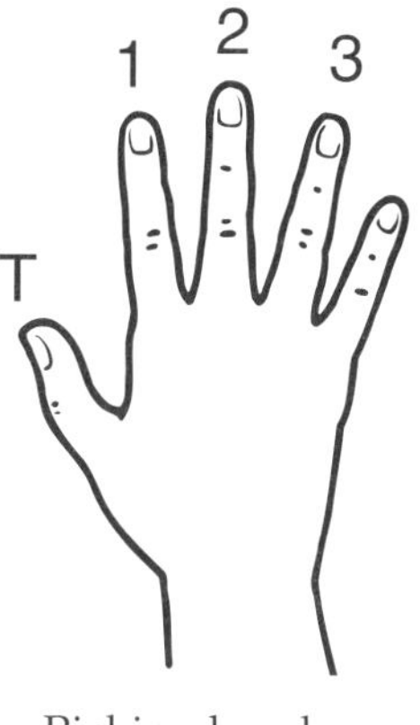

Picking hand

G7 CHORD 

Let's learn another dominant seventh chord: G7. This looks similar to the G chord, but the triangle shape points the other way.

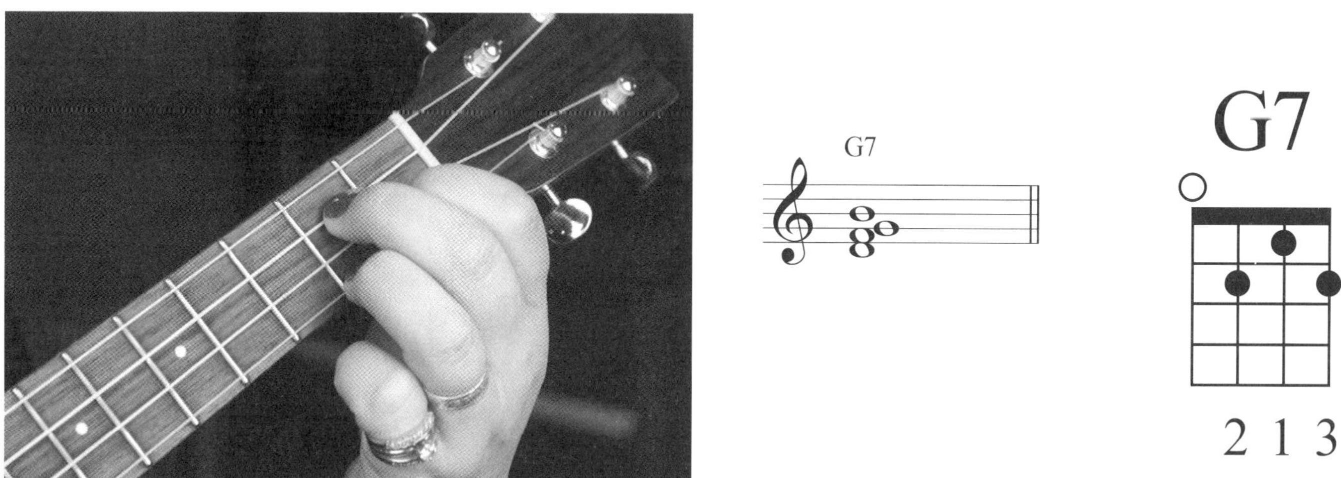

And now let's try using G7 in a fingerpicking exercise with C and F chords. We're playing eighth notes here, but the fingerpicking order (T–1–2–3) is the same. We'll call this Fingerpicking Pattern 1.

Exercise 2: Fingerpicking Pattern 1

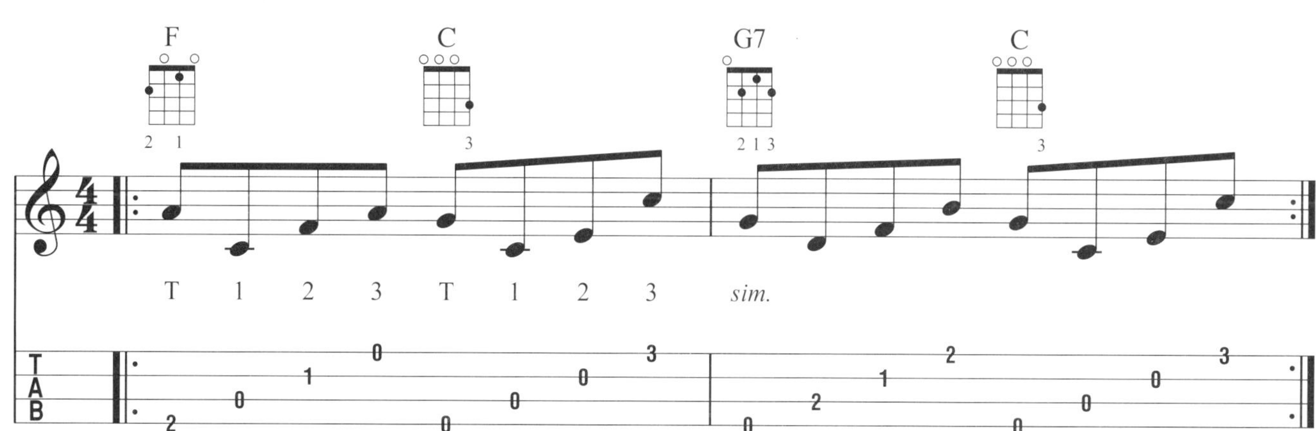

With the new G7 chord, we can now play the first two verses of "Can't Help Falling in Love" using Fingerpicking Pattern 1.

CAN'T HELP FALLING IN LOVE

from the Paramount Picture BLUE HAWAII

Words and Music by George David Weiss, Hugo Peretti and Luigi Creatore

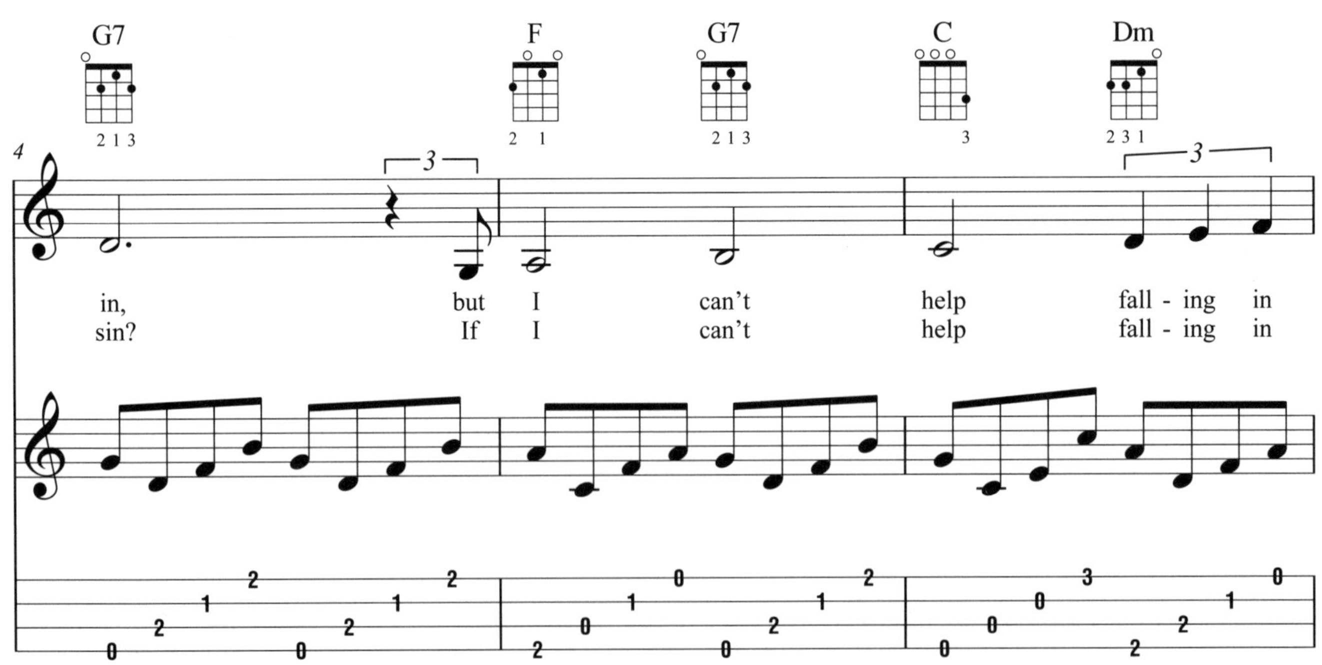

Let's try another arpeggio fingerpicking pattern now. In this one, we'll be plucking two strings at once. The pattern will be T–1–2/3–1. Try it out with Am and F chords. We'll call this Fingerpicking Pattern 2.

Exercise 3: Fingerpicking Pattern 2

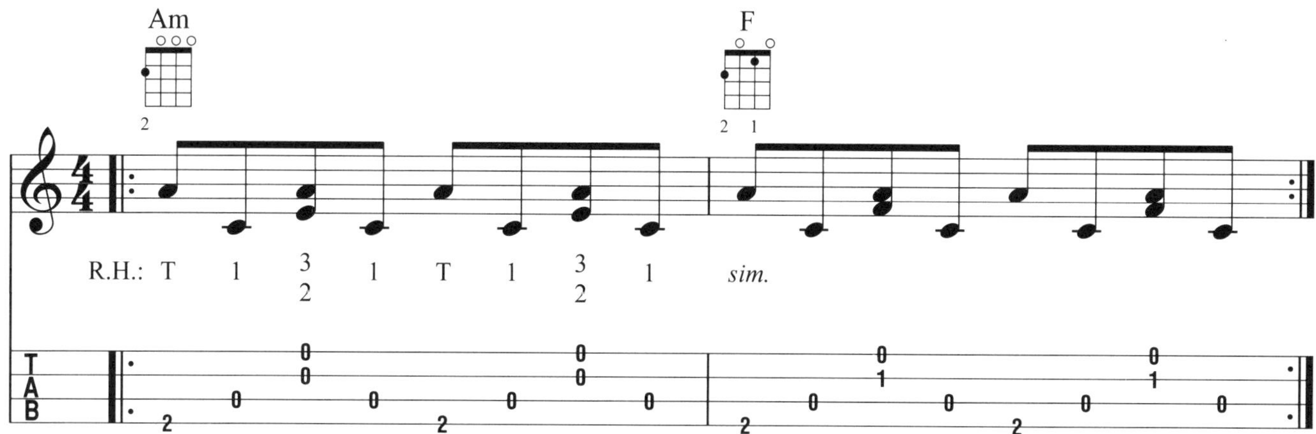

TAKE YOUR TIME!

When playing arpeggios like this, you don't have to finger the entire chord right away. Since you're not playing all the notes at once—like you do when strumming—you can plant the fingers one or two at a time if you need to.

Fingerpicking Pattern 2 sounds a bit like something a pianist might play. Let's try it in another exercise using four chords: G–C–E7–F.

Exercise 4

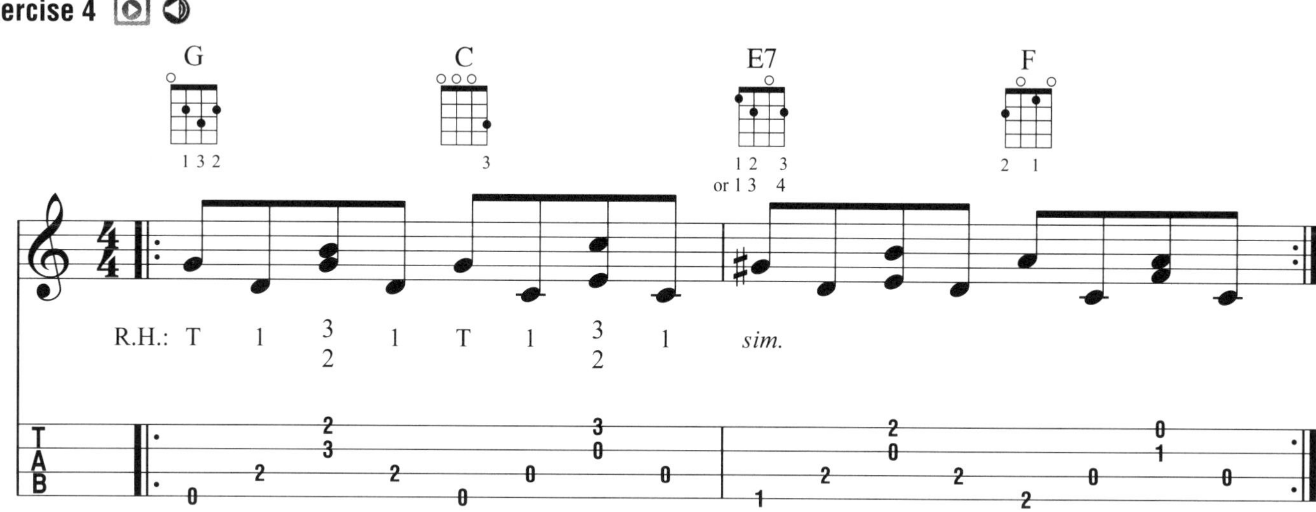

Let's use Fingerpicking Pattern 2 to play "Winter Song" by Sara Bareilles and Ingrid Michaelson!

WINTER SONG

Words and Music by Sara Bareilles
and Ingrid Michaelson

G
1 3 2
8
sea.
told.
way.
My voice, a bea - con in the
They say we're bur - ied far
I'll be your har - ves - ter of
C
3
F
2 1
Am
2
10
night.
light
My words will be your light to car - ry you to
just like a dis - tant star I sim - ply can - not
and send it out to - night so we can start a -
F
2 1
12
me.
hold.
gain.
Is love a - live? Is love
Is love a - live? Is love
Is love a - live? Is love

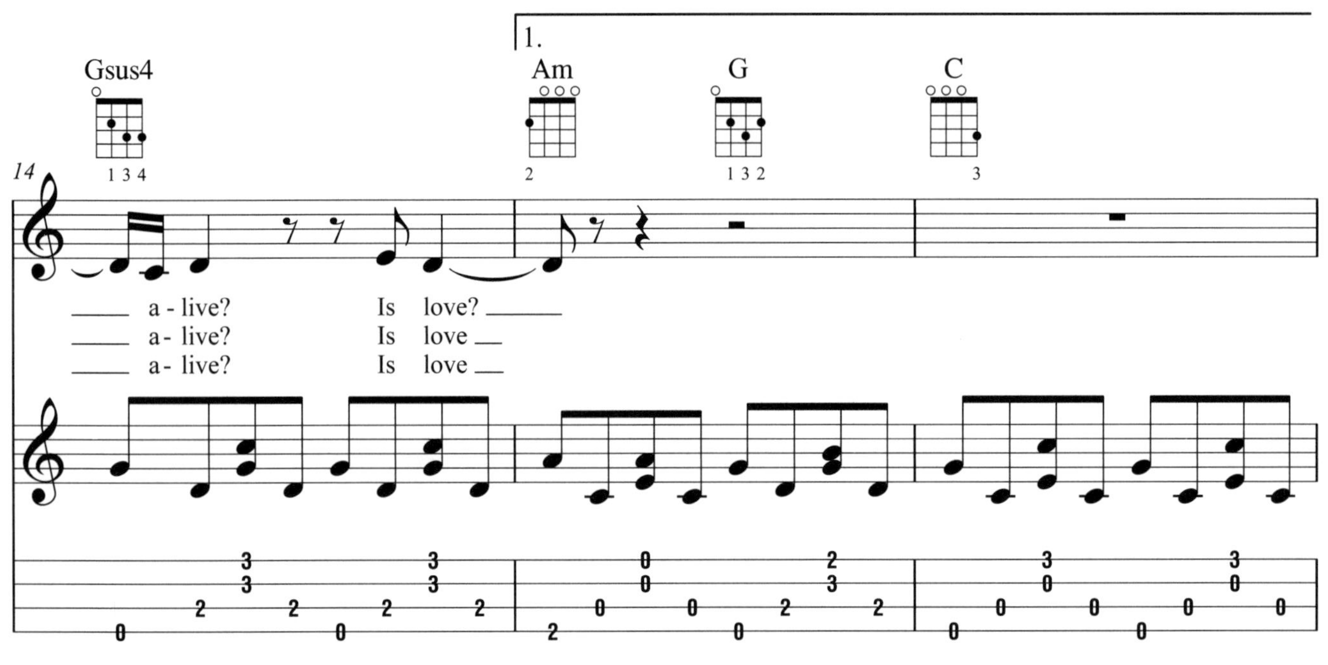
1.
Gsus4
Am
G
C
1 3 4
2
1 3 2
3
a - live?
Is
love?
a - live?
Is
love
a - live?
Is
love

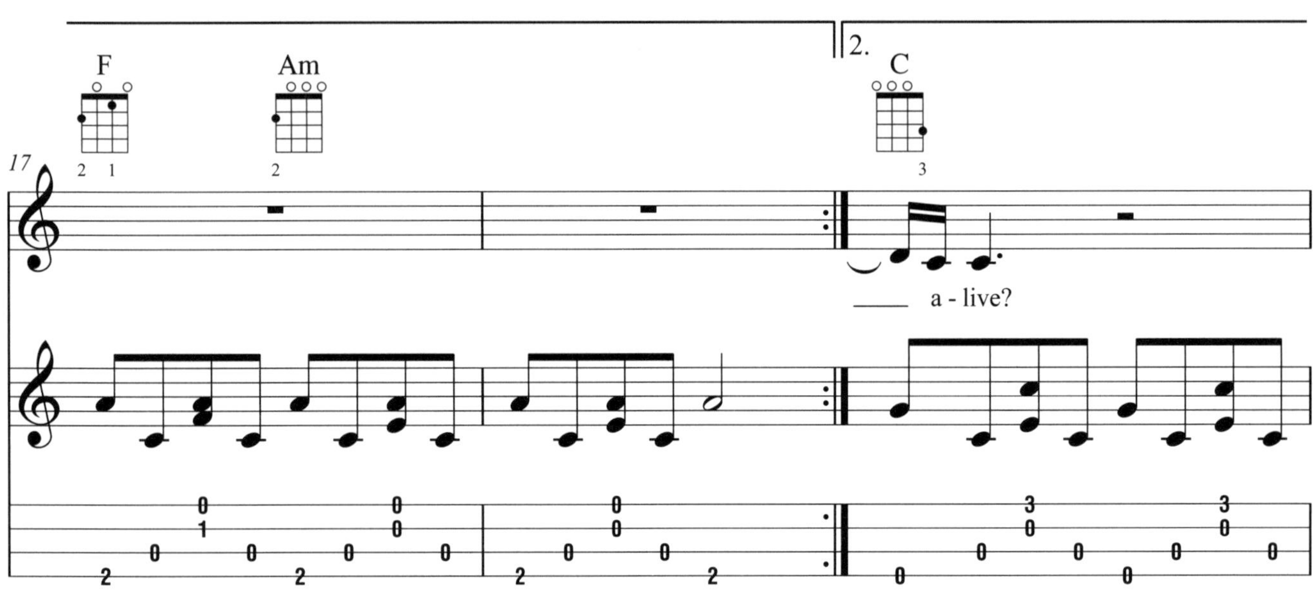
F
Am
2.
C
2 1
2
3
a - live?

Chorus
Am
E7
2
1 2 3
or 1 3 4
This
is
my
win -

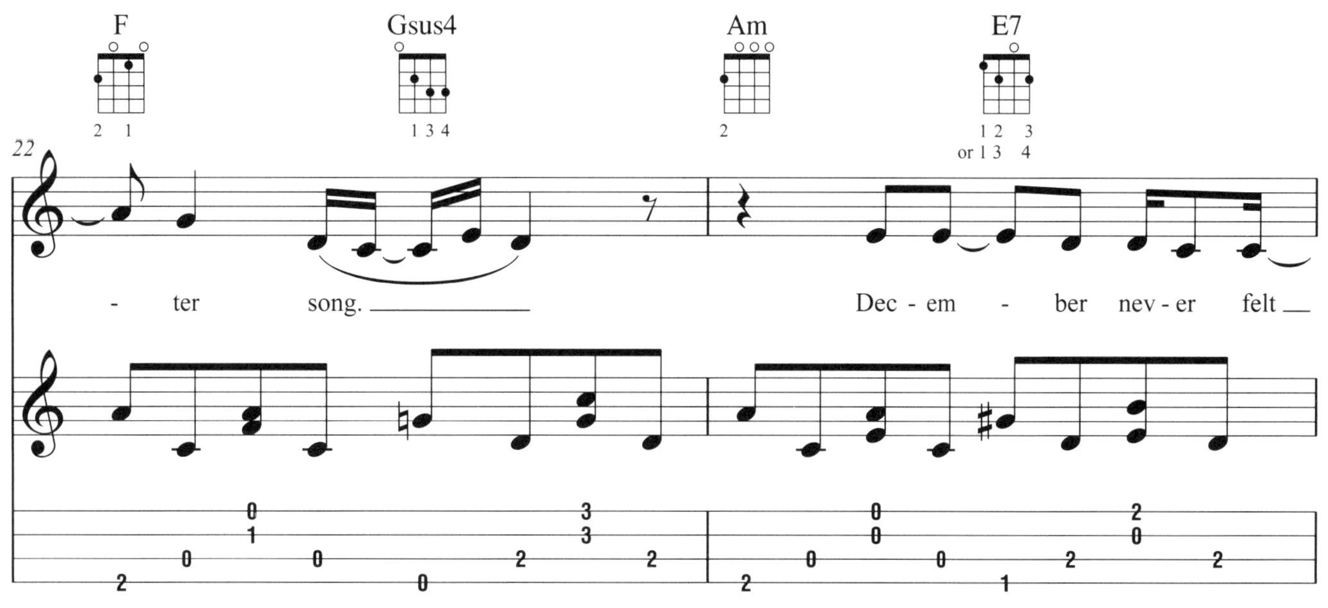
F
Gsus4
Am
E7
22
- ter song.
Dec - em - ber nev - er felt

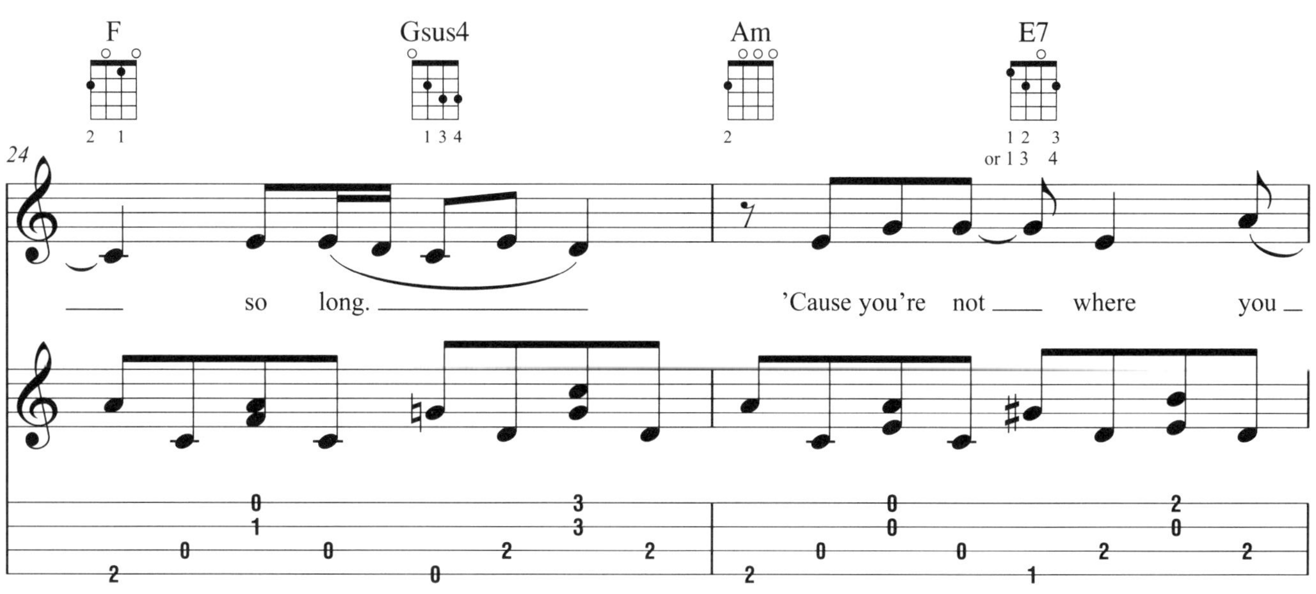
F
Gsus4
Am
E7
24
so long.
'Cause you're not where you

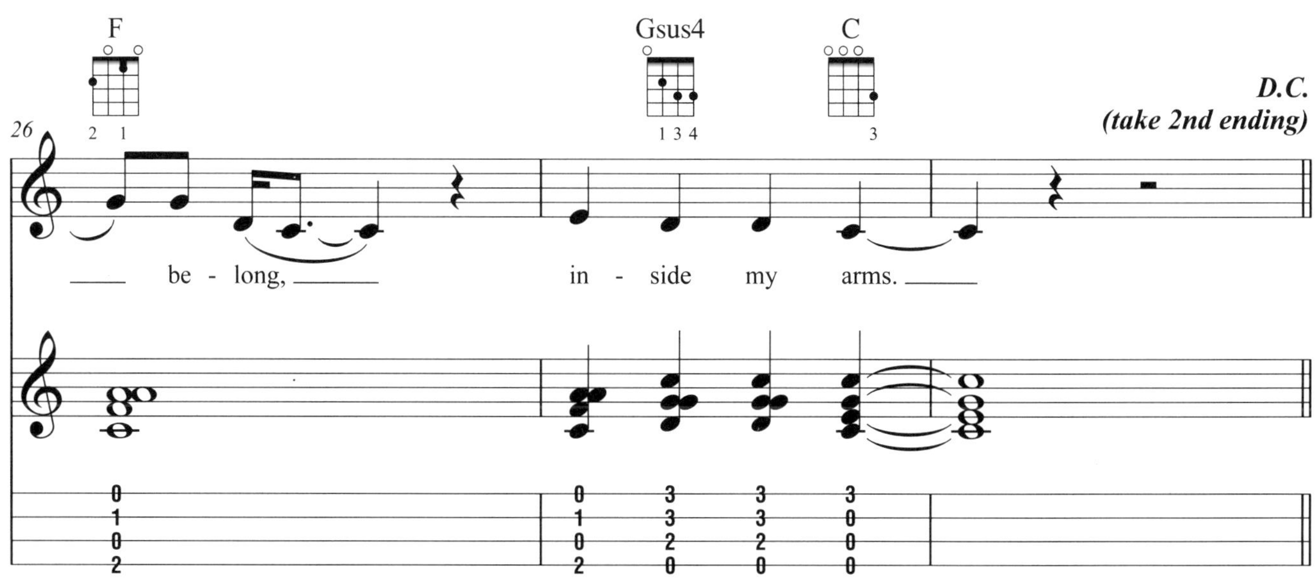
F
Gsus4
C
D.C.
(take 2nd ending)
26
be - long,
in - side my arms.

B♭maj7 CHORD

Let's learn another major seventh chord: B♭maj7. We'll need this chord to play "All Is Found."

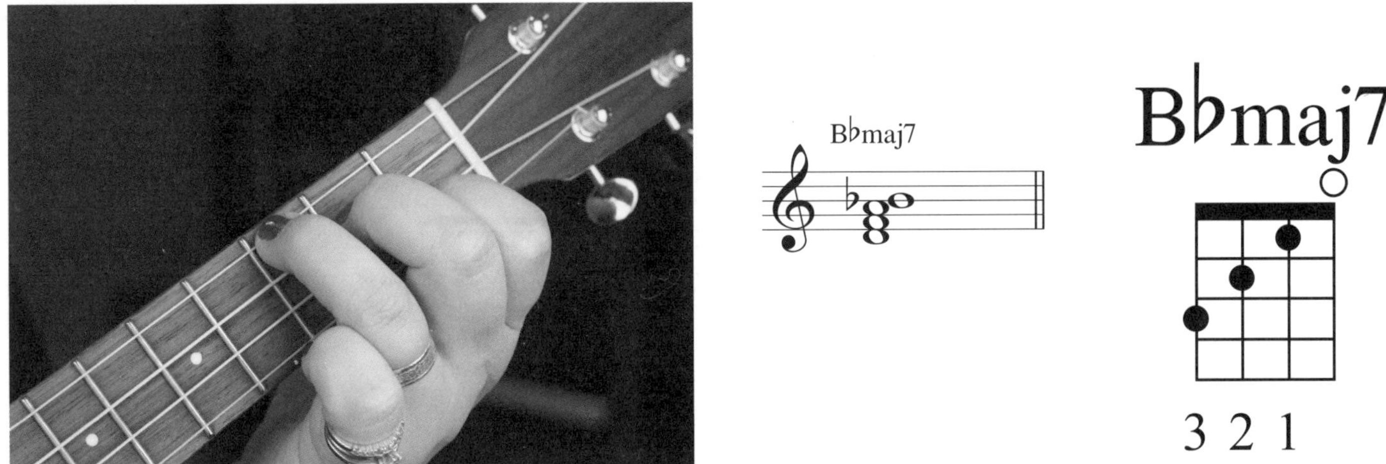

ALTERNATING THUMB STYLE (TRAVIS PICKING)

Another common fingerpicking style is called the *alternating thumb* style. It's very similar to a style of fingerpicking on guitar called *Travis picking*.

Let's start by alternating your thumb between open strings 3 and 4 in quarter notes, like this:

Exercise 5

Now we'll add the first and second fingers between the thumb notes to complete the pattern. Plant your first (index) finger on string 2 and your second (middle) finger on string 1. With your thumb planted on string 3, your picking hand should look like this:

Now, slowly try the exercise. We'll call this Fingerpicking Pattern 3.

Exercise 6: Fingerpicking Pattern 3

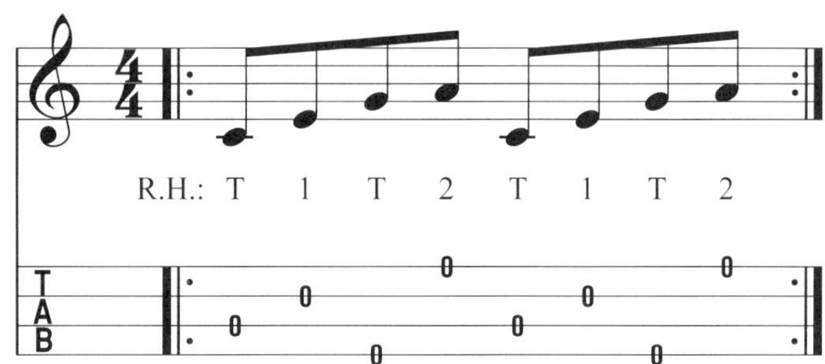

You can really get this pattern moving quickly with some practice!

Once you get the hang of it, let's try moving between a few chords. We'll use an F chord with our new B♭maj7 chord. On the fretting hand, keep your first finger on fret 1 of string 2 the whole time since it's used in both chords.

Exercise 7

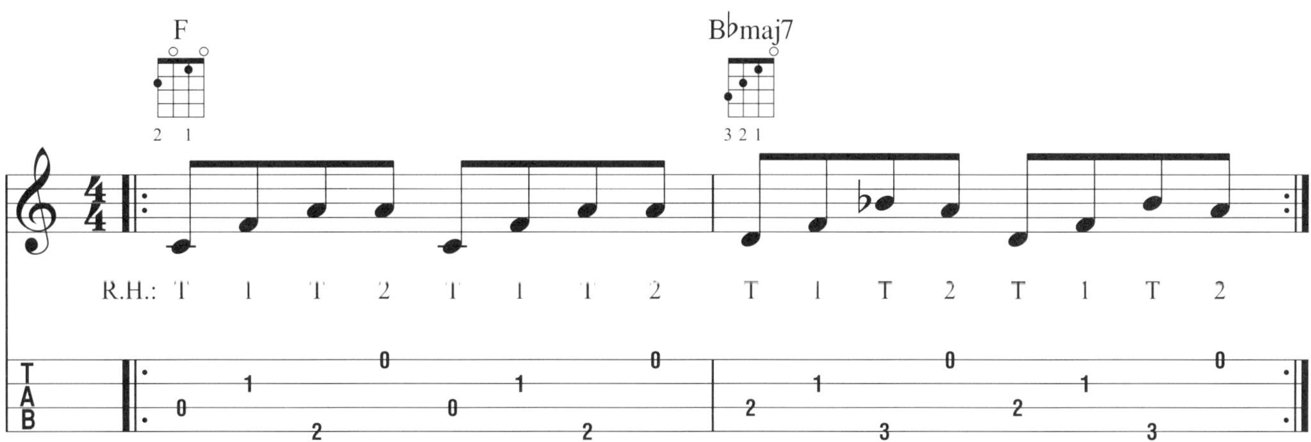

Now let's switch between Dm and B♭maj7. We'll pick up the tempo here. Again, the fretting-hand first finger can remain on fret 1 of string 2 the whole time.

Exercise 8

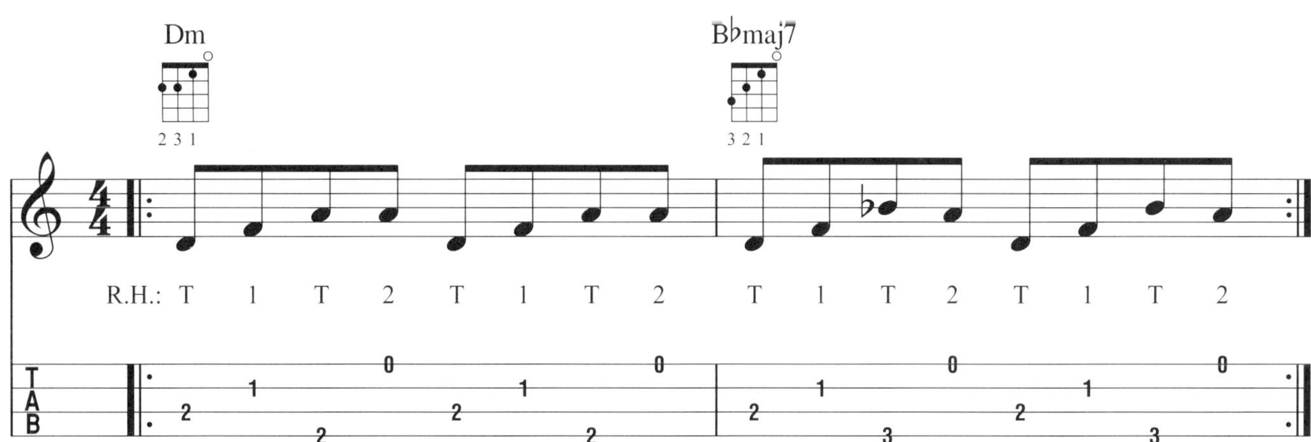

All right, now let's use Fingerpicking Pattern 3 to play "All Is Found." Watch for the new B♭maj7 chord in the chorus! Also, you'll see "*rit.*" At the very end. This stands for the Italian term *ritardando*, which means "gradually slowing down."

ALL IS FOUND

from FROZEN 2

Music and Lyrics by Kristen Anderson-Lopez
and Robert Lopez

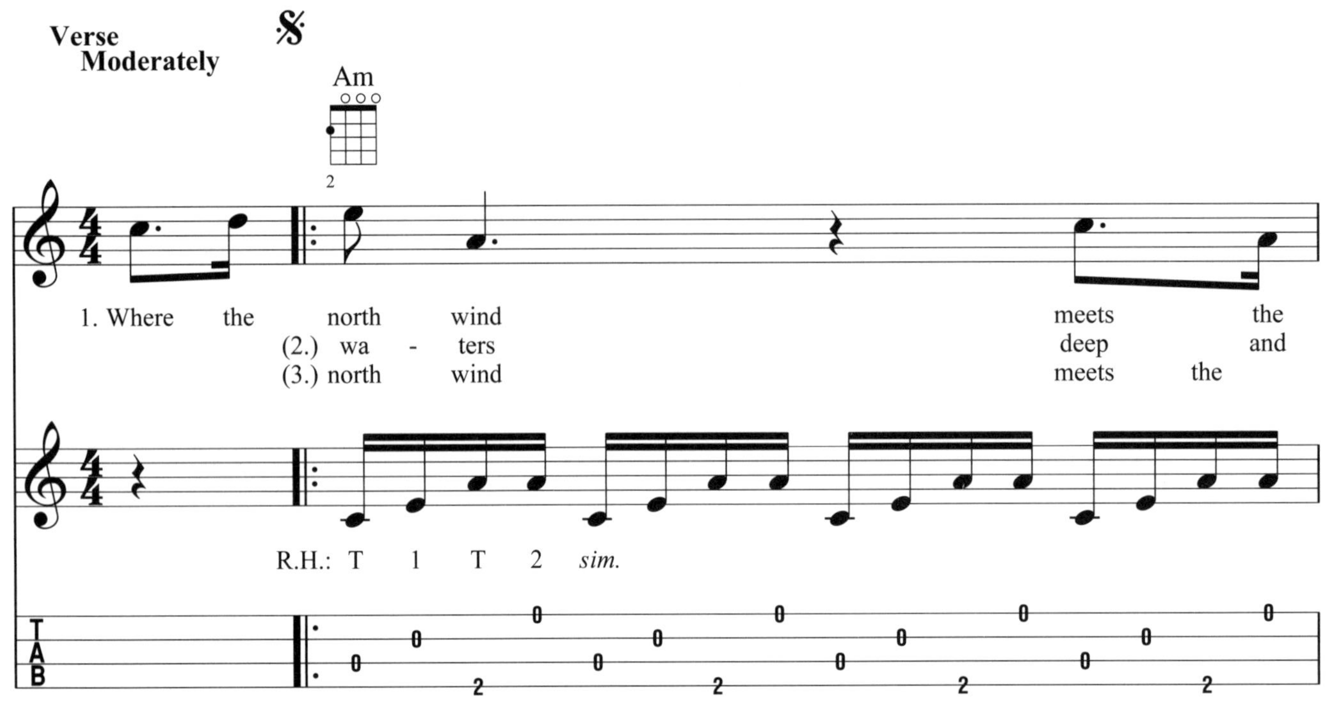

To Coda
C
Dm
F
memory. Sleep my darling, safe and sound,
Dive down deep into her sound.
memory. Come, my
G
1.
Am
for in this river all is found. 2. In her
But not too far, or you'll be
2.
Am
Bridge
F
drowned. Yes, she will sing to those who

C
Dm
3
2 3 1
10
hear, and in her song, all mag - ic

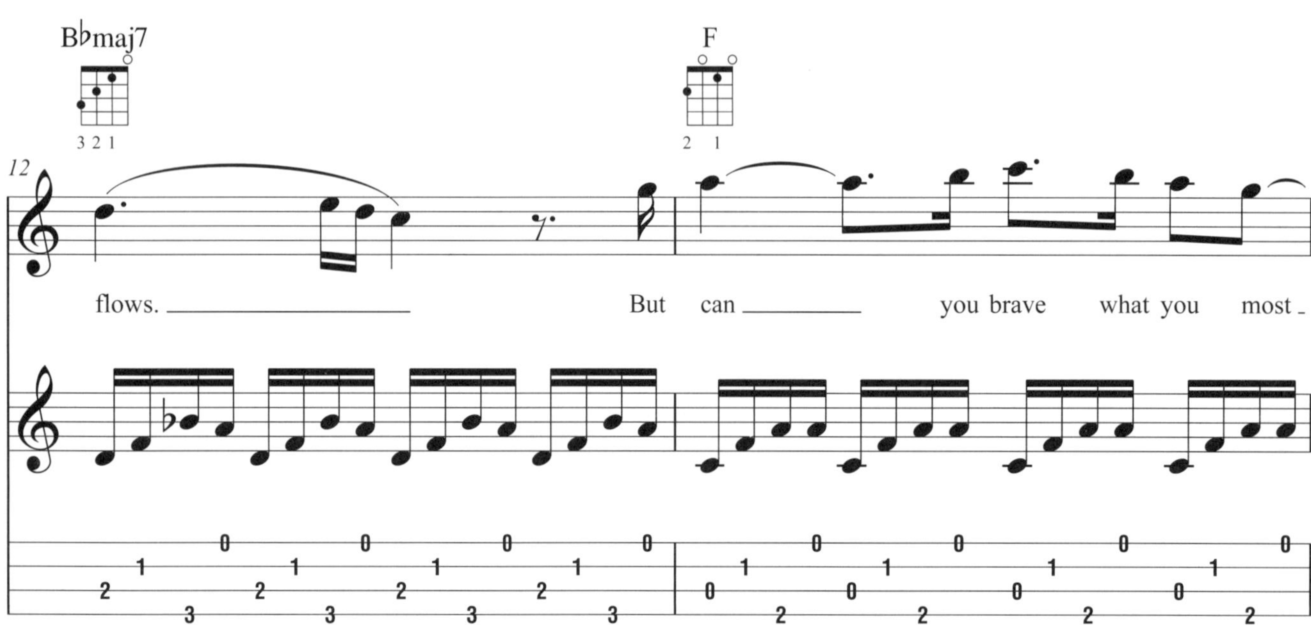
B♭maj7
F
3 2 1
2 1
12
flows. But can you brave what you most

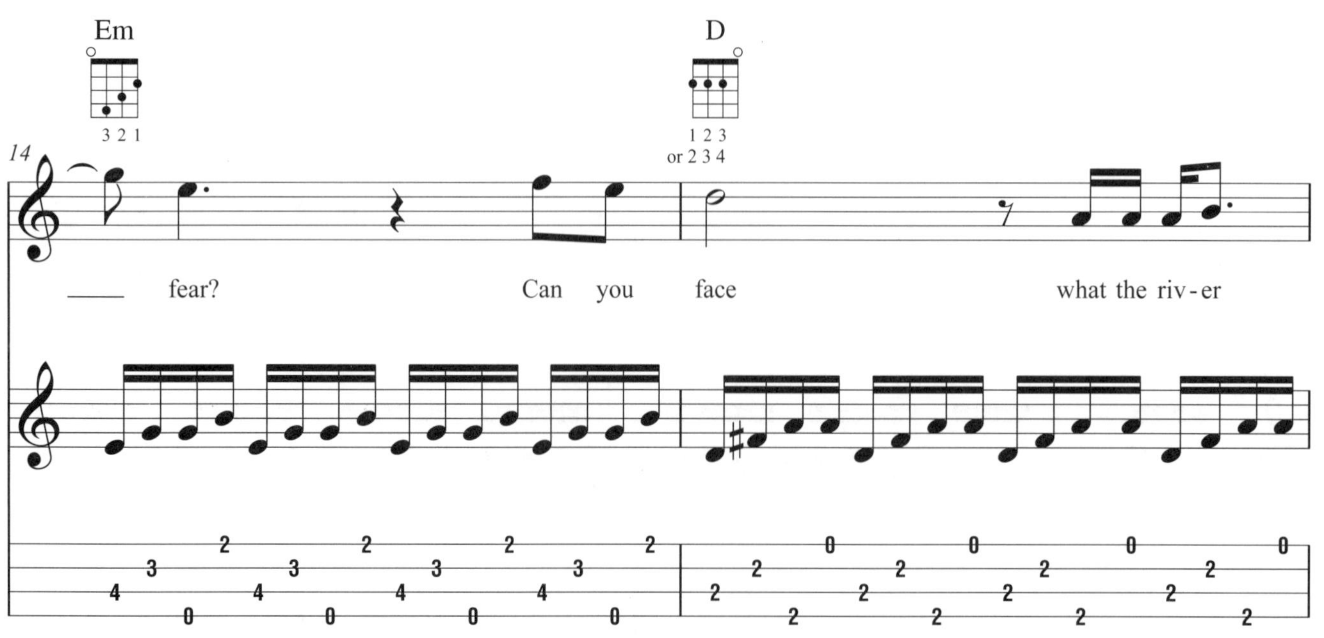
Em
D
3 2 1
1 2 3
or 2 3 4
14
fear? Can you face what the riv - er

Coda
F
Dm
D.S. al Coda
knows? 3. Where the
dar - ling, home - ward
bound: when all is
lost, then all is
Outro
Am
Em
found. All is found. All is
F
G

ROLLING PATTERN

For the next song, Adele's "Someone Like You," we just need to learn one more chord and one more arpeggio fingerpicking pattern. This pattern is sometimes called a "rolling pattern" because of its gentle, rolling motion. We're only going to be using strings 3–1 here:

- The thumb plays all the notes on string 3.
- The index finger plays all the notes on string 2.
- The middle finger plays all the notes on string 1.

We're going to play this pattern in 16th notes: ♬♬. Remember, there are two 16th notes for each eighth note. We count them by saying, "1-e-&-a, 2-e-&-a," etc.

We'll call this Fingerpicking Pattern 4. Here's the basic technique with a G chord:

Exercise 9: Fingerpicking Pattern 4

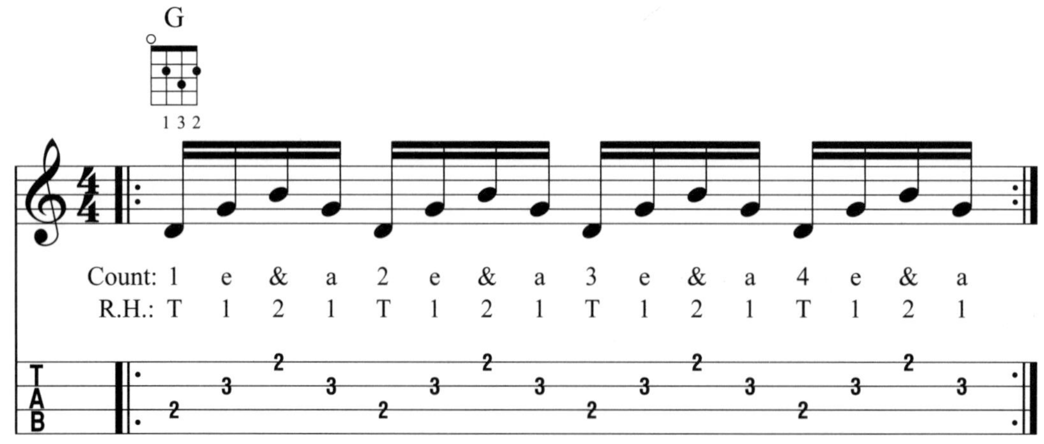

Bm CHORD

This is a three-string version of Bm. You may notice that it's just like Gmaj7, only without the G string. The "X" in the chord grid tells you not to play that string.

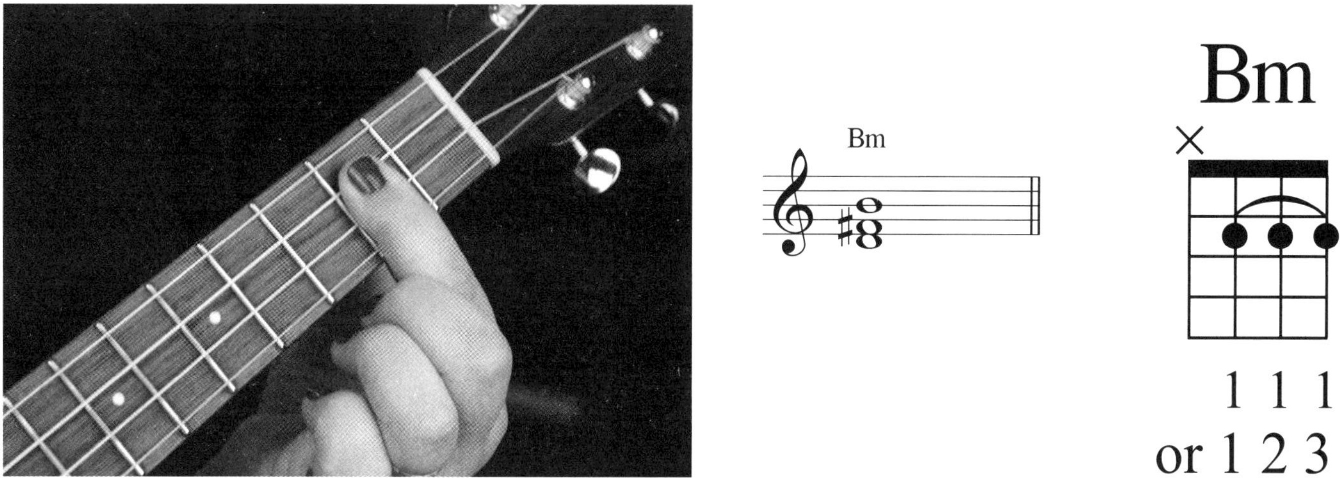

Try going back and forth between G and Bm chords with Fingerpicking Pattern 4.

Exercise 10

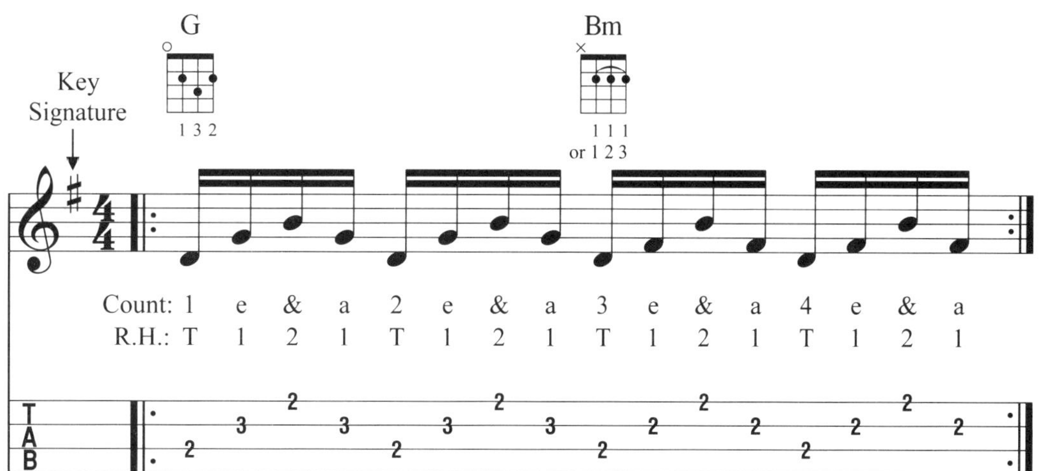

KEY SIGNATURES

Notice the sharp symbol (#) on the F line in Exercise 10. This is called a *key signature*, and it tells you to play every F note as F#—in other words, one fret higher than F—throughout the whole song.

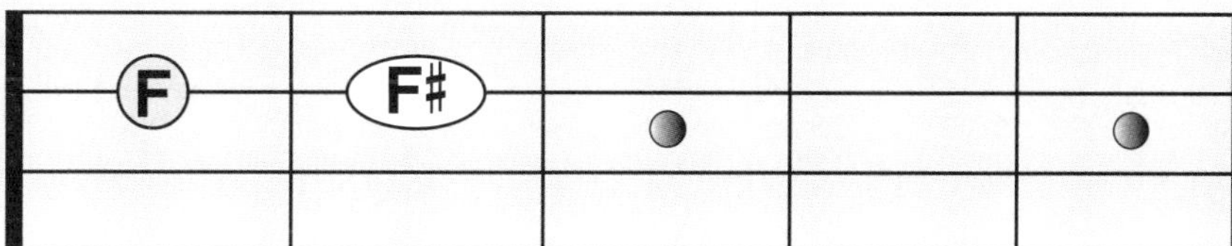

Now let's put the new Bm chord and Fingerpicking Pattern 4 to use with "Someone Like You."

FIRST TIME ONLY

Notice the "Play first time only" direction within the bracket during the verse. This tells you to play this part only the first time through. On the repeat of the verse, you just skip over this bracket entirely. (Basically, there's an extra line of lyrics in the first verse that doesn't show up in the second verse!)

D.S. AL FINE

This is similar to the "D.S. al Coda" direction we saw in the song "Brave." But this time, once you go back to the sign, you play until you see "Fine," which means "end."

SOMEONE LIKE YOU

Words and Music by Adele Adkins
and Dan Wilson

Em
C
found a girl and you're mar-ried now.
yes - ter-day was the time of our lives. We were

G
Bm
I heard that your dreams came true. Guess she
born and raised in a sum-mer haze, bound

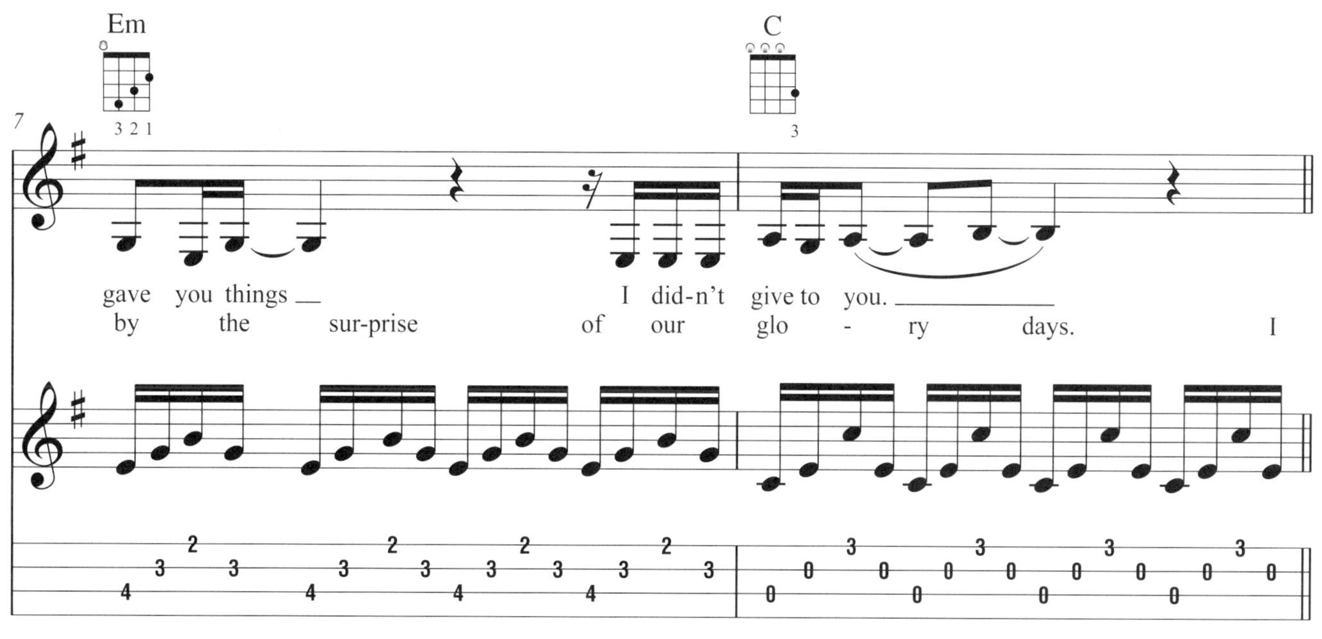
Em
C
gave you things I did-n't give to you.
by the sur-prise of our glo - ry days. I

Play 1st time only
G
Bm
Old friend, why are you so shy? Ain't like
Em
C
you to hold back, or hide from the light. I
Pre-Chorus
D
Em
hate to turn up out of the blue un - in - vit - ed, but I

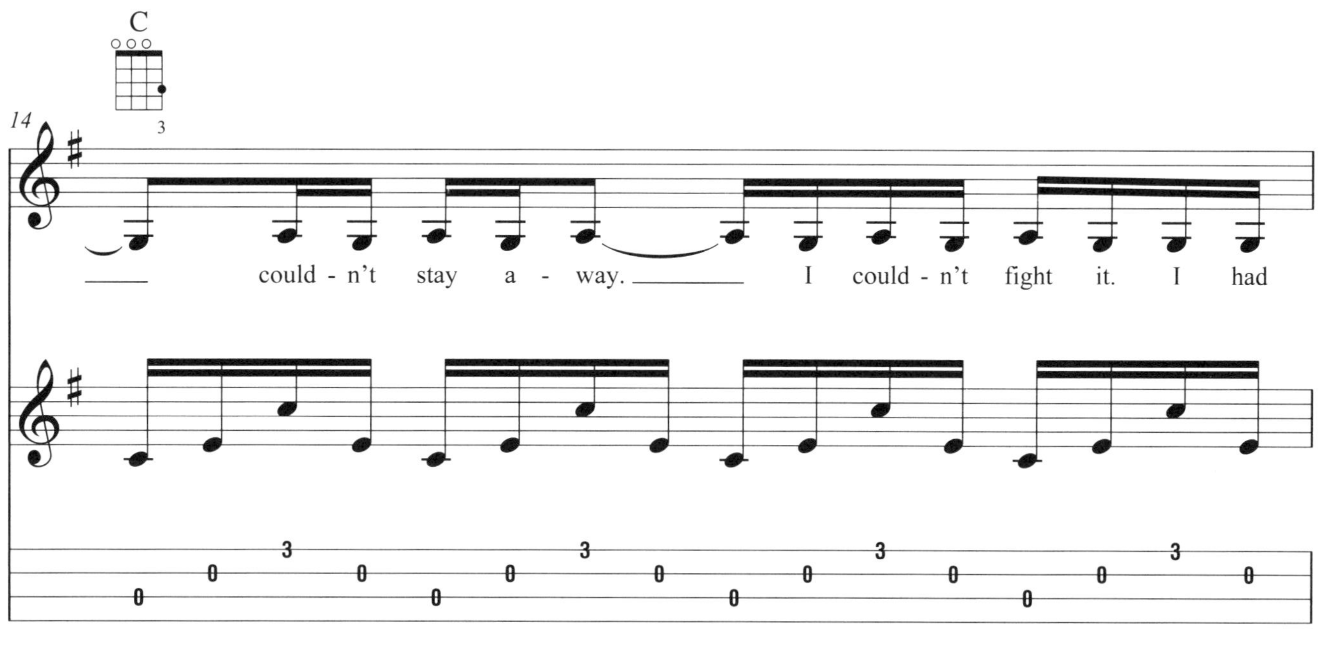
C
14
could - n't stay a - way. I could - n't fight it. I had

D
Em
15
hoped you'd see my face and that you'd be re - mind - ed that for

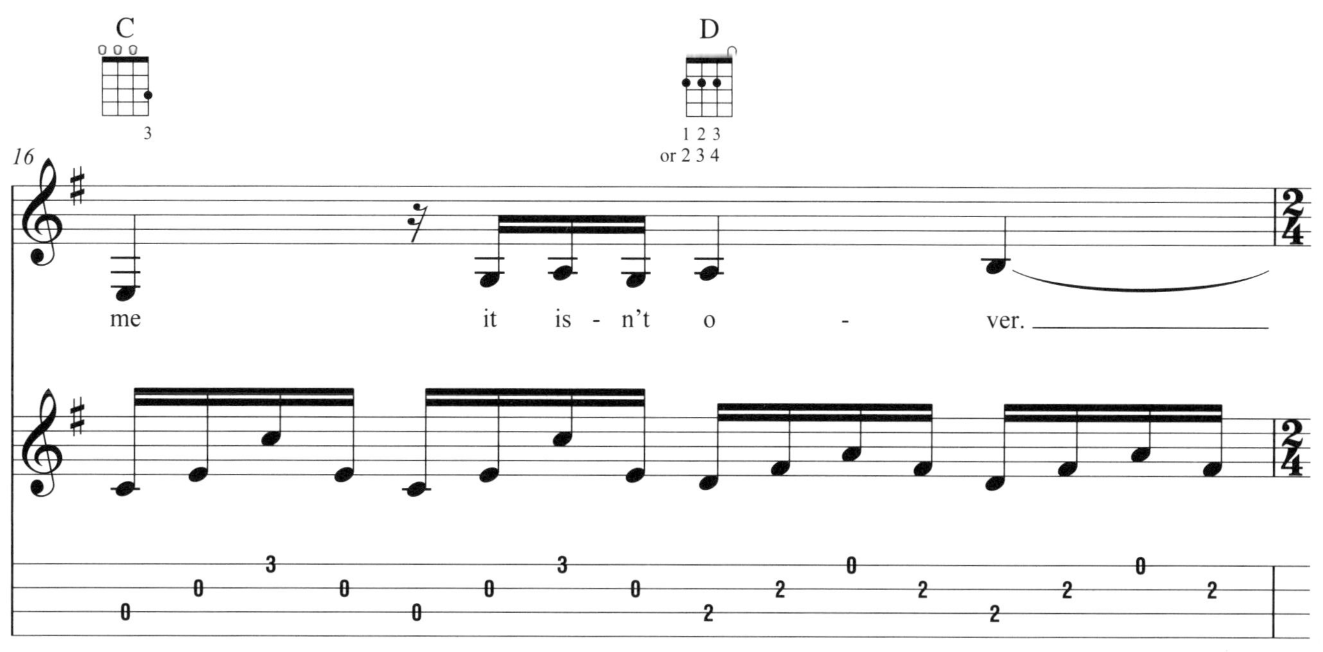
C
D
16
me it is - n't o - ver.

Chorus
C
G
D
3
1 3 2
1 2 3
or 2 3 4
Nev-er mind, I'll find some-one like
Em
C
G
D
3 2 1
you.
I wish noth-ing but the best for
you two. Don't for - get me, I beg. I'll re -

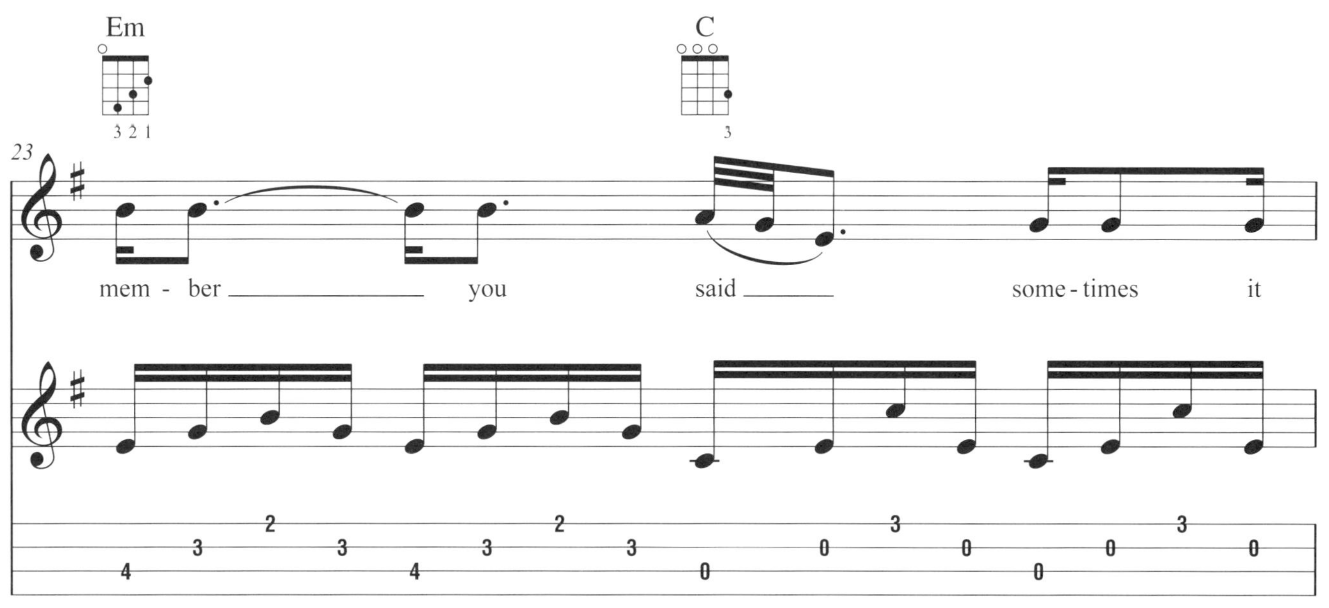
Em
3 2 1
C
3
23
mem - ber you said some - times it

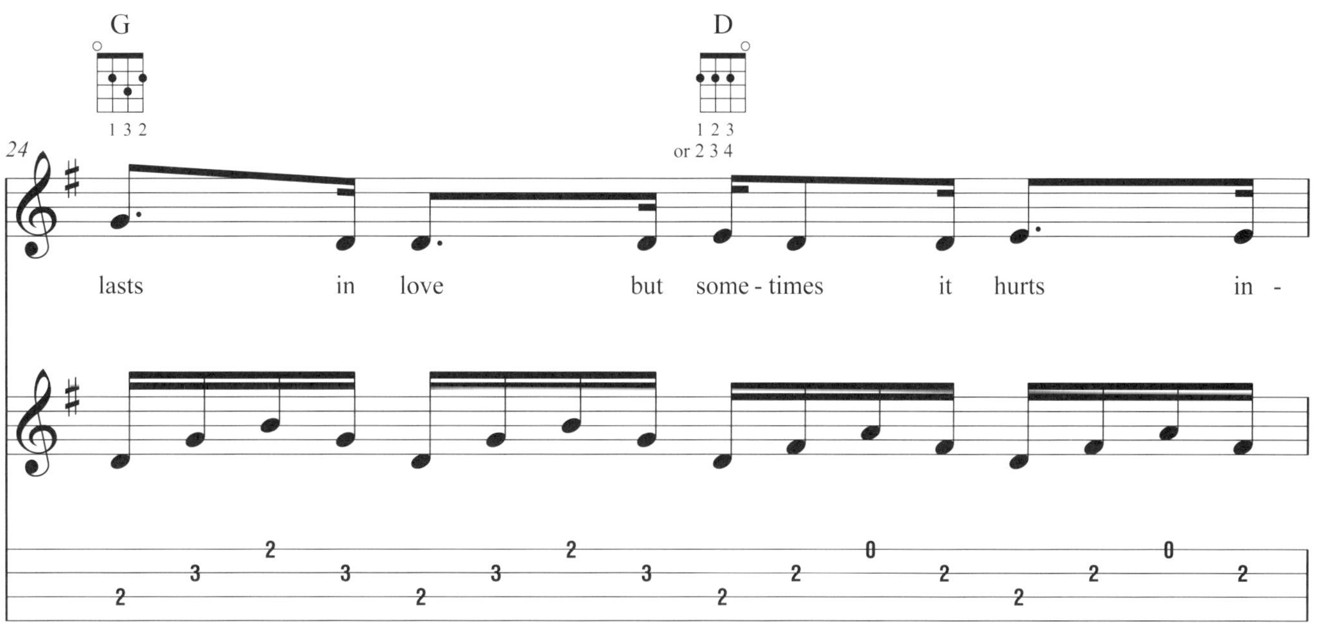
G
1 3 2
D
1 2 3
or 2 3 4
24
lasts in love but some - times it hurts in -

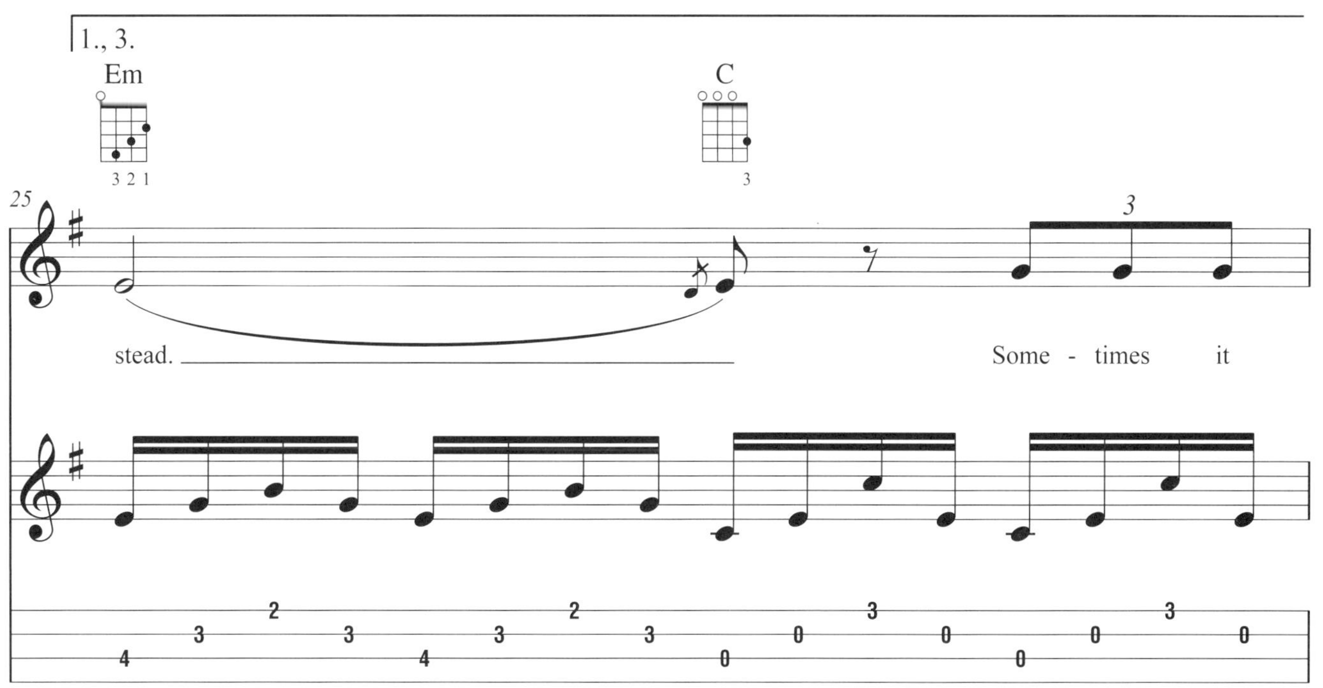
1., 3.
Em
3 2 1
C
3
25
stead. Some - times it

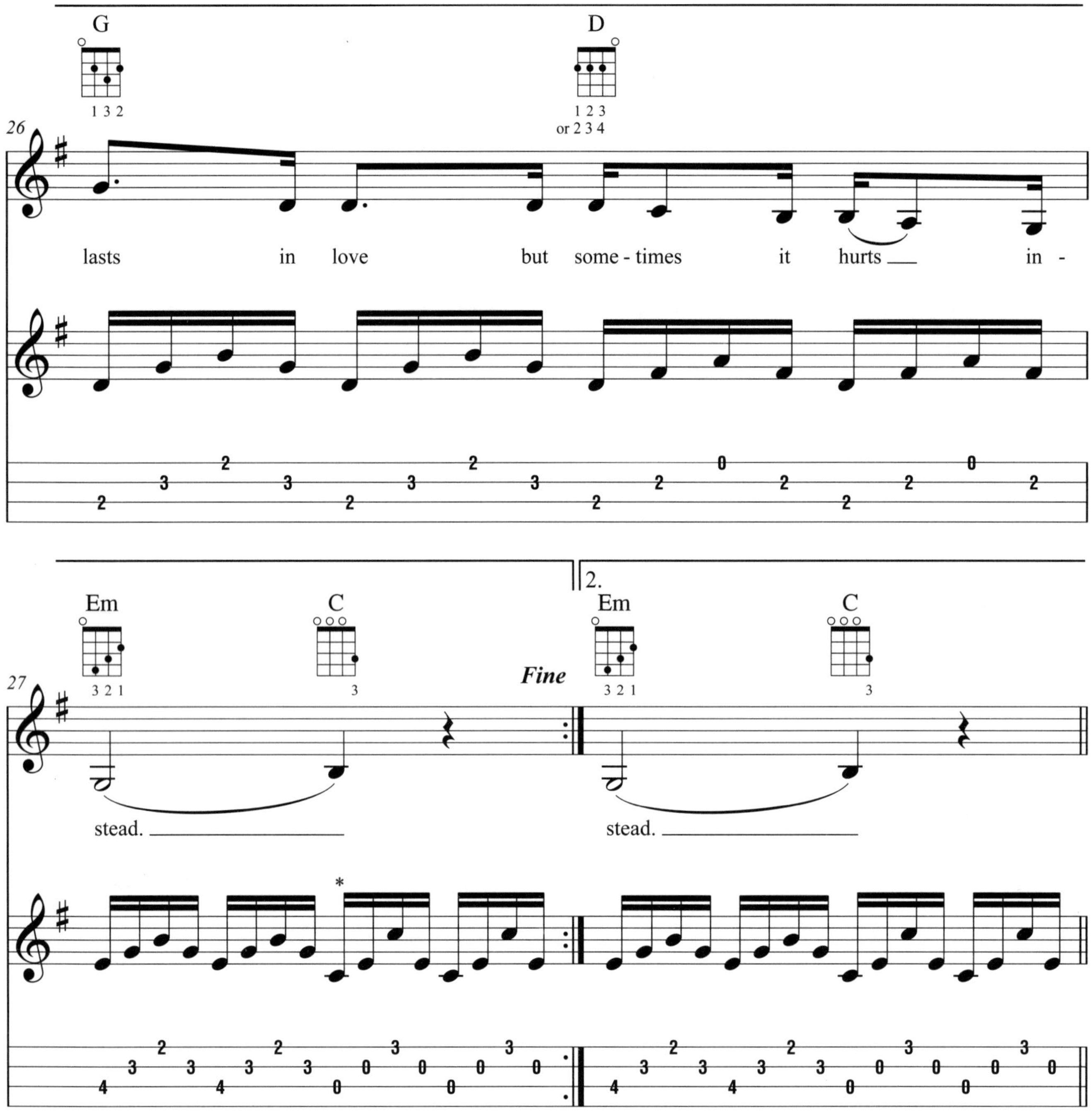

G D

26

lasts in love but some - times it hurts in -

Em C | 2. Em C

27

Fine

stead. stead.

* For final bar of song, end with strummed C chord on beat 3.

Bridge

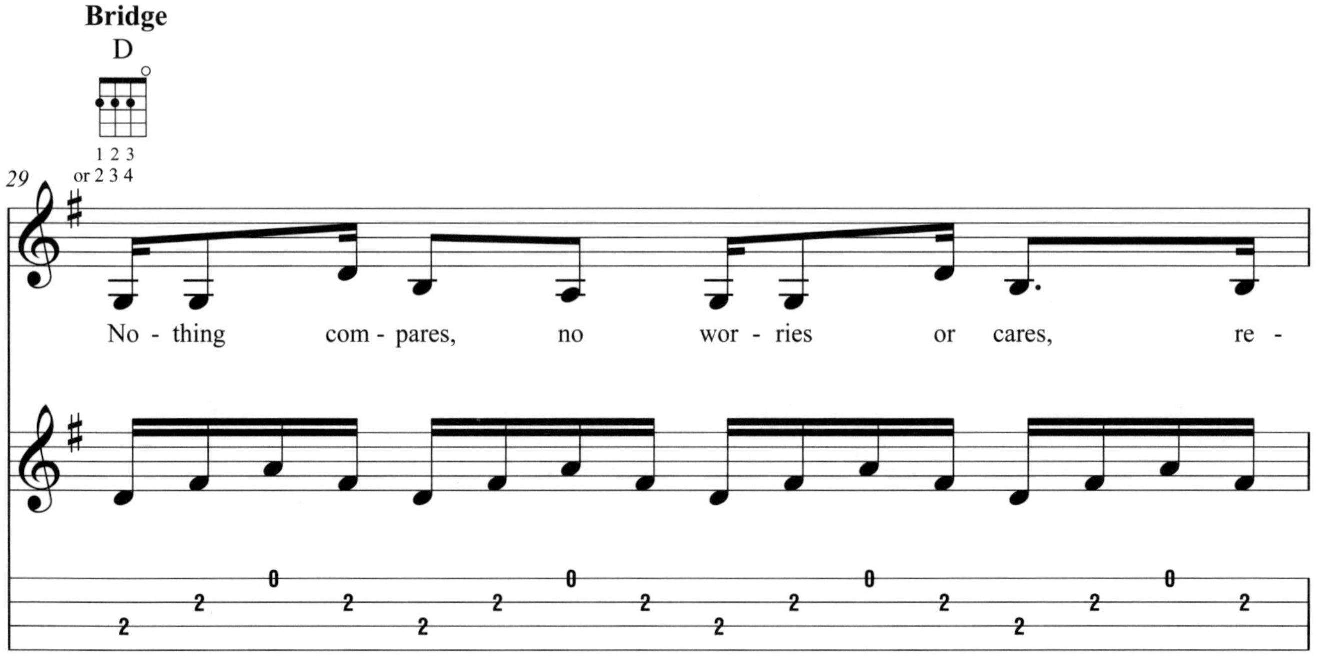

Em
3 2 1
grets and mis - takes, they are mem - o - ries made.

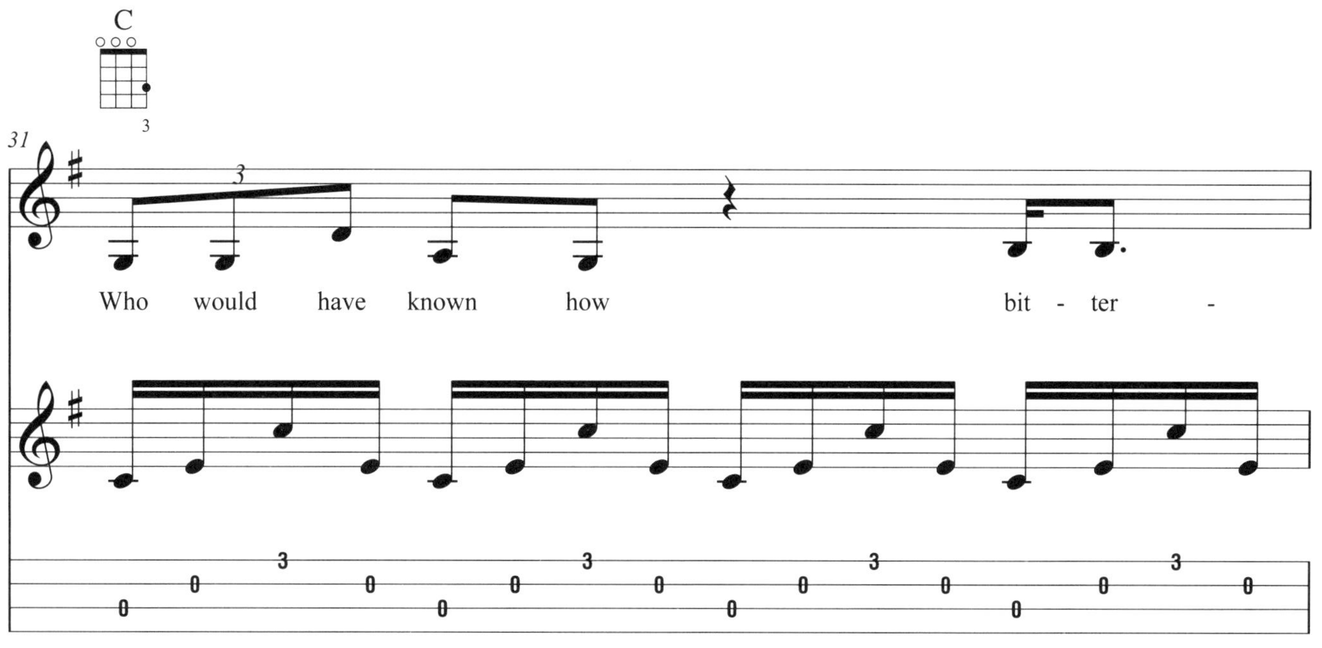
C
3
Who would have known how bit - ter -

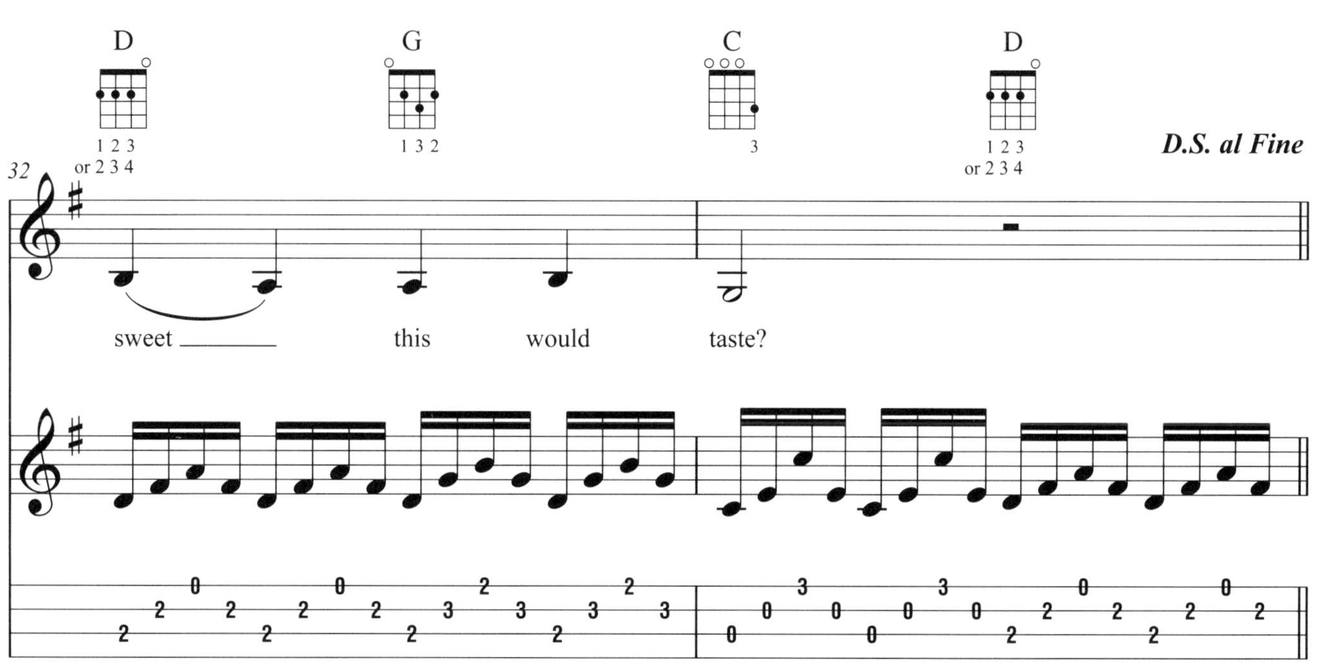
D
1 2 3
or 2 3 4
G
1 3 2
C
3
D
1 2 3
or 2 3 4
D.S. al Fine
sweet this would taste?

We'll close out with Leonard Cohen's "Hallelujah," which is in 6/8 meter and uses a variation of the rolling pattern with the thumb, first, second, and third fingers. Instead of a four-note pattern that uses three strings, it's a six-note pattern that uses all four strings. On a C chord, it'll look like this:

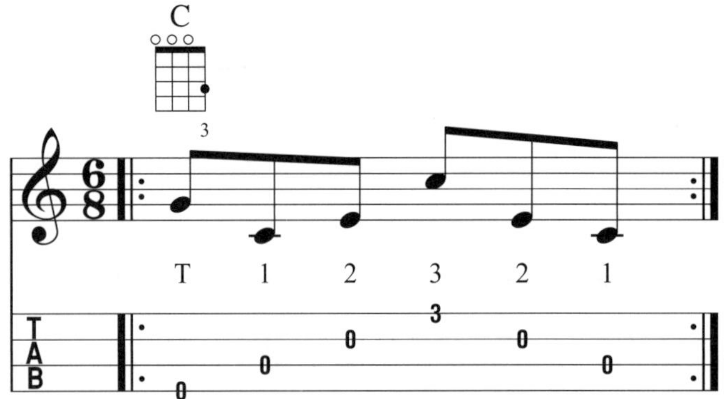

Now let's use this new pattern on "Hallelujah."

HALLELUJAH

Words and Music by Leonard Cohen

Verse
Moderately

C Am C

1. Well, I heard there was a se - cret chord _ that Da - vid played and it
(2.) faith was strong but you need - ed proof. _ You saw her bath - ing
3. Ba - by, I've been here be - fore. I've seen this room _ and I've
4. May - be there's a God a - bove, but all I've _ ev - er

4

Am F G

pleased the Lord, but you don't _ real - ly care for mu - sic,
on the roof, her beau - ty and the moon - light o - ver -
walked this floor. You know, I used to live a - lone _ be - fore I
learned from love was how to _ shoot some - bod - y who out -

C
G
C
do ya? Well, it goes like this: the
threw ya. She tied you to the
knew ya. And I've seen your flag on the
drew ya. And it's not a cry that you
F
G
Am
F
fourth, the fifth, the mi - nor fall and the ma - jor lift, the
kitch - en chair. She broke your throne and she cut your hair, and
mar - ble arch, and love is not a vict - 'ry march. It's a
hear at night. It's not some - bod - y who's seen the light. It's a
G
E7
Am
baf - fled king com - pos - ing Hal - le - lu - jah.
from your lips she drew the Hal - le - lu - jah.
cold and it's a bro - ken Hal - le - lu - jah.
cold and it's a bro - ken Hal - le - lu - jah.

Chorus
F
Am
16
Hal - le - lu - jah. Hal - le - lu - jah.
F
20
Hal - le - lu - jah. Hal - le -
1., 2., 3.
C
G
C
23
lu - jah.

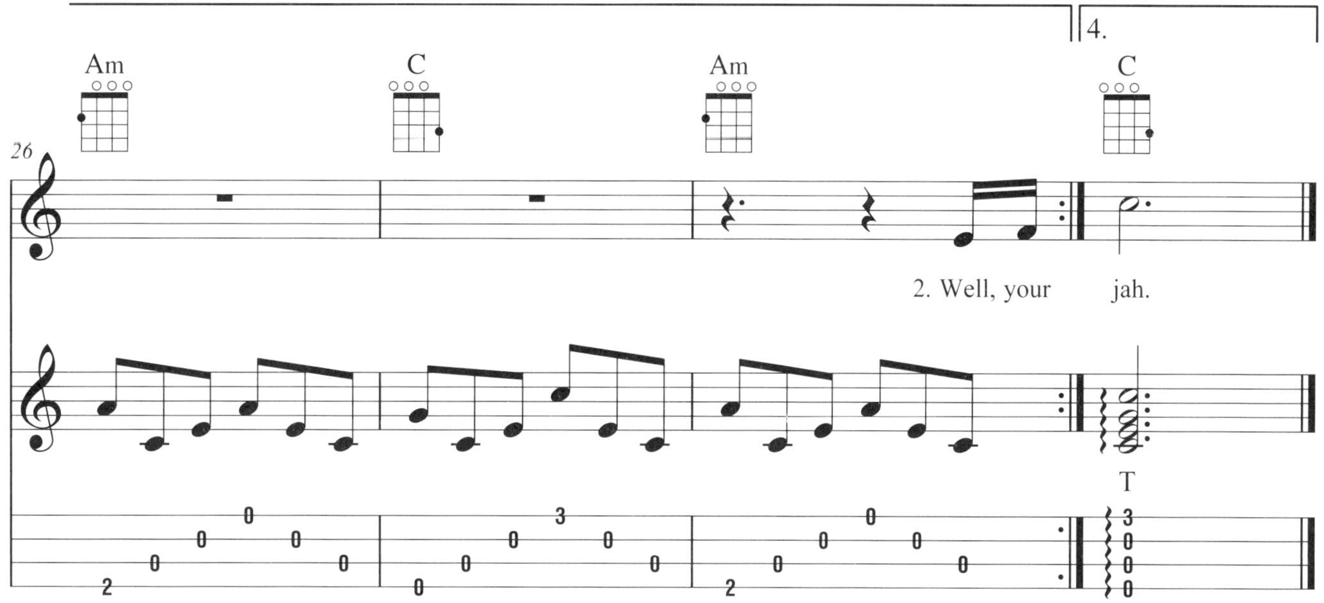

CHAPTER REVIEW

Here's what we learned in the final chapter:

- Three new chords: **G7**, **B♭maj7,** and **Bm.**
- **Basic fingerpicking technique** using the thumb, index, middle, and ring fingers on the plucking hand.
- An **arpeggio** is the notes of a chord played separately instead of all together.
- Several arpeggio **fingerpicking patterns.**
- **Alternating thumb style (Travis picking)** patterns involve rocking the thumb back and forth between two strings while filling in the gaps with the index and middle fingers.
- Five songs: **"Can't Help Falling in Love," "Winter Song," "All Is Found," "Someone Like You"** and **"Hallelujah."**
- **Tablature** (or "**tab**," for short) is another type of notation that tells you what frets and strings to play on the ukulele.
- When playing arpeggios, you don't always have to fret the chord all at once.
- The term **ritardando** (**rit.**) means to gradually slow down.
- **16th notes** are twice as fast as eighth notes and are counted "1-e-&-a, 2-e-&-a," etc.
- A **key signature** tells you to play certain notes as sharps or flats every time you see them in a song.
- **D.S. al Fine** tells you to go back to the D.S. sign and play until you see "Fine."

CHORD APPENDIX

For quick reference, here are all the chords you learned in this book.

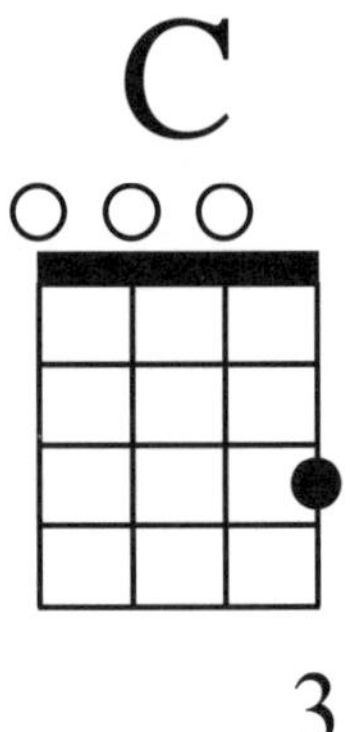

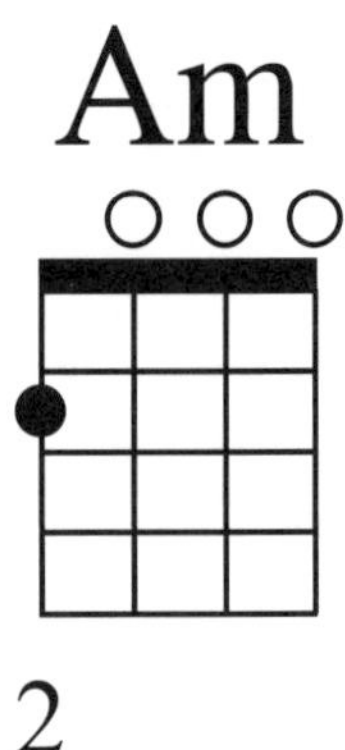

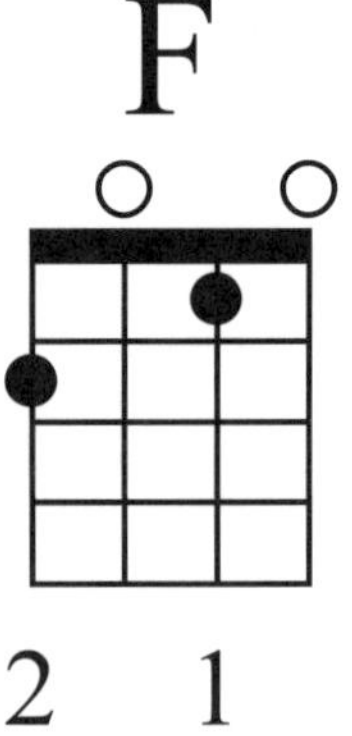

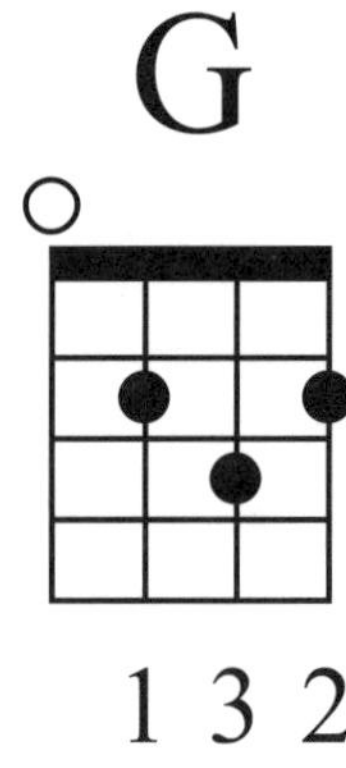

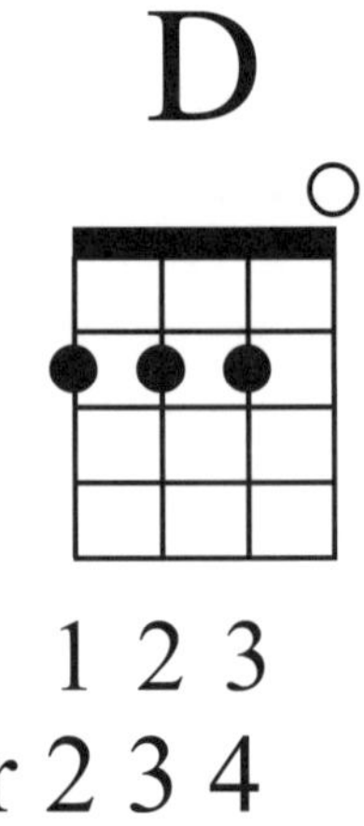

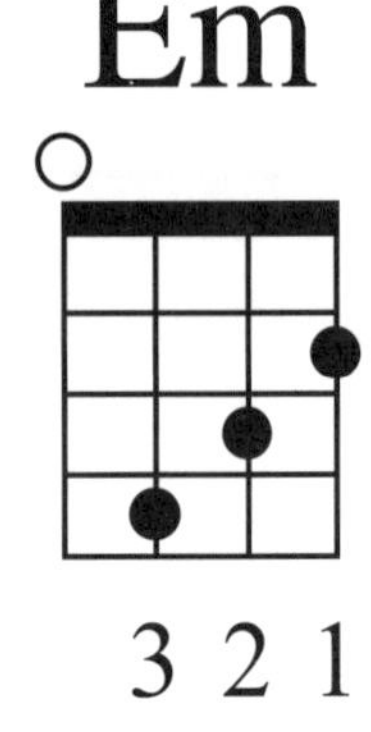

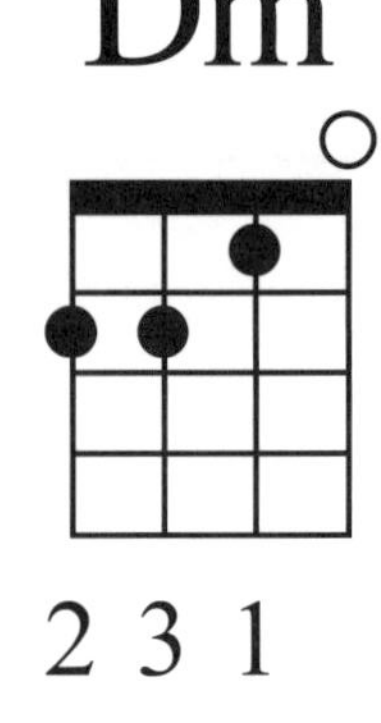

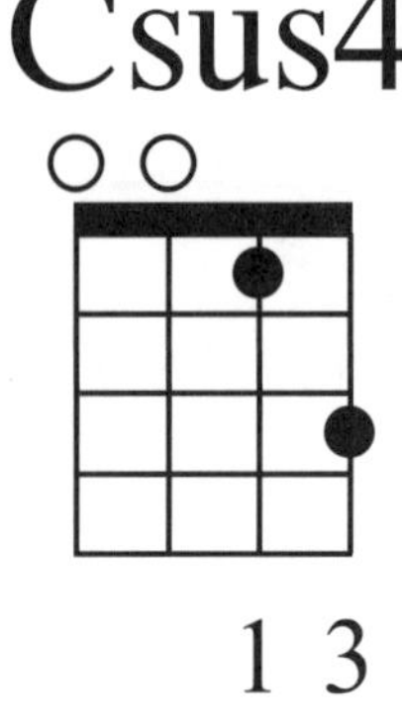

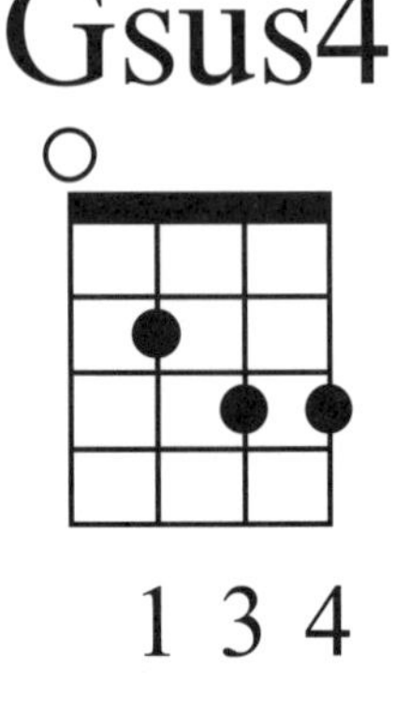

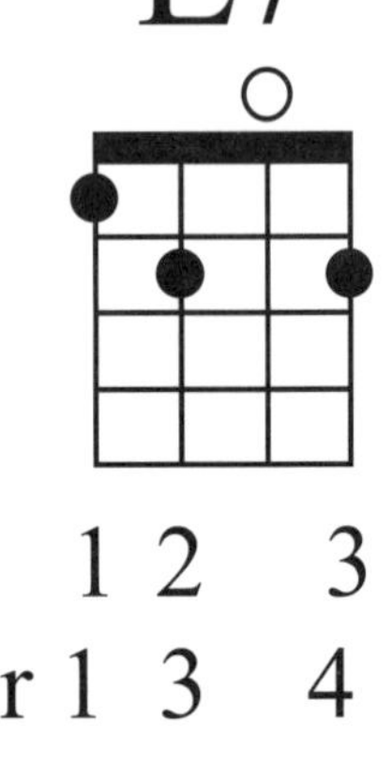

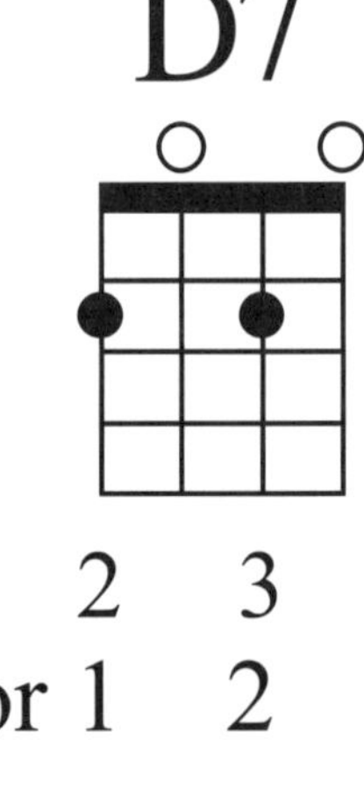

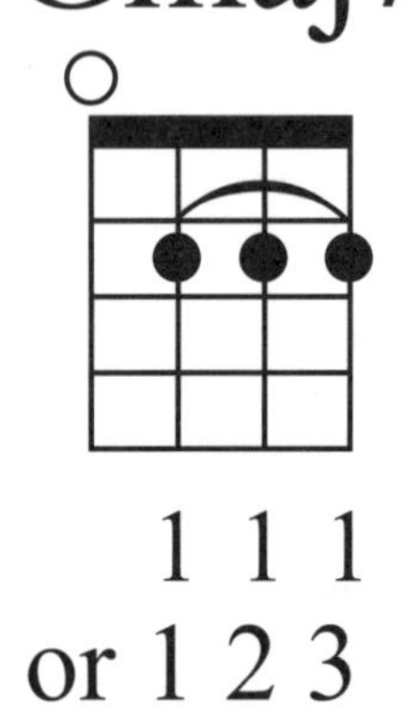

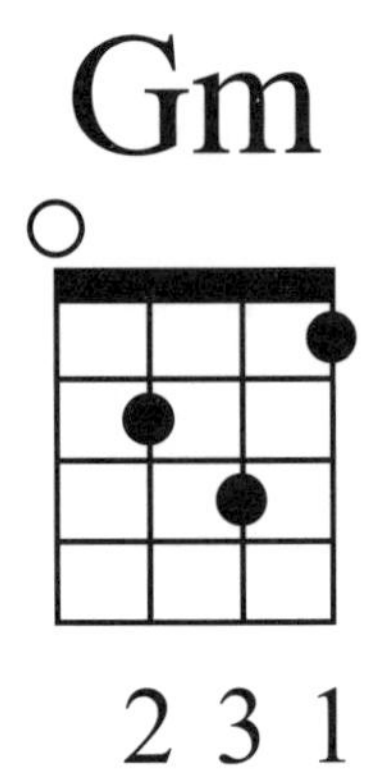

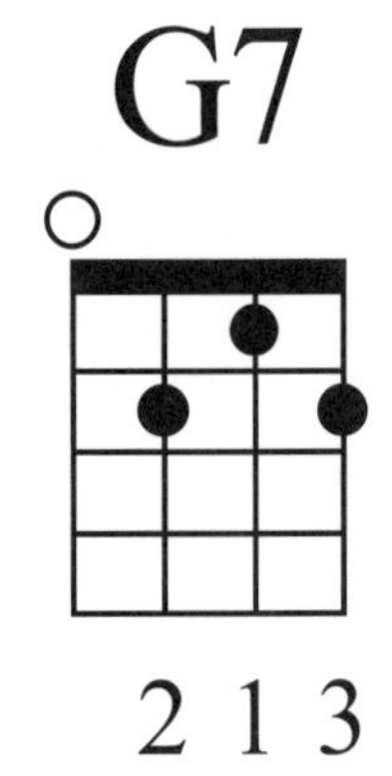

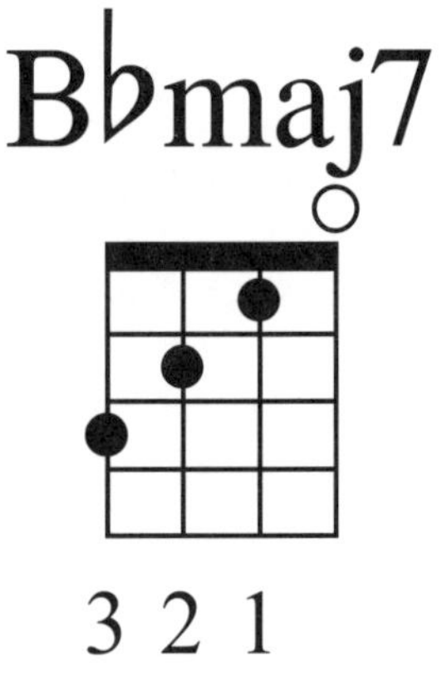

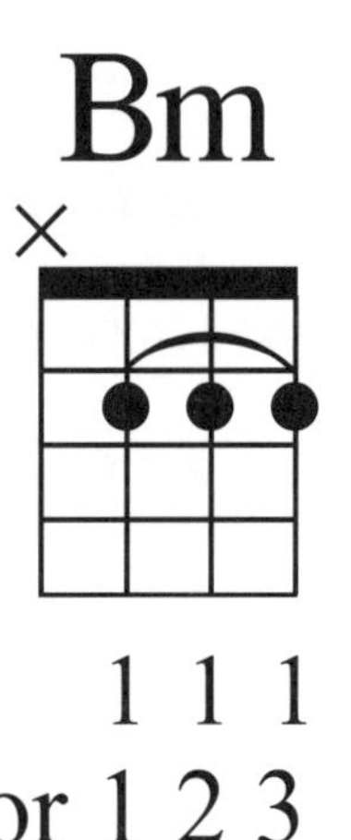

And here are several more chords to work on. You'll find these used in lots of songs!

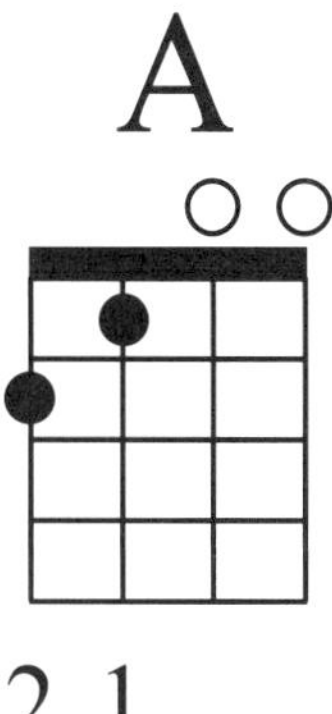

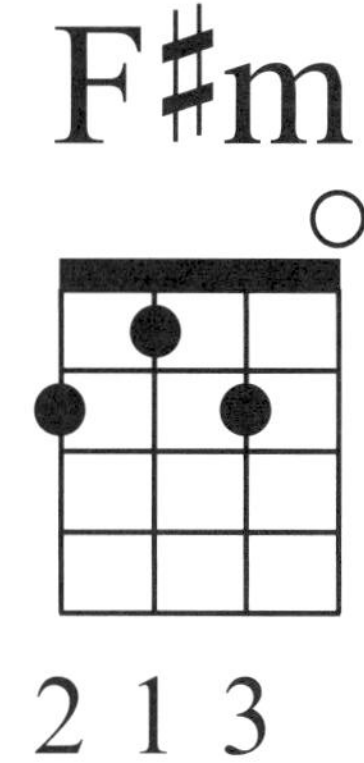

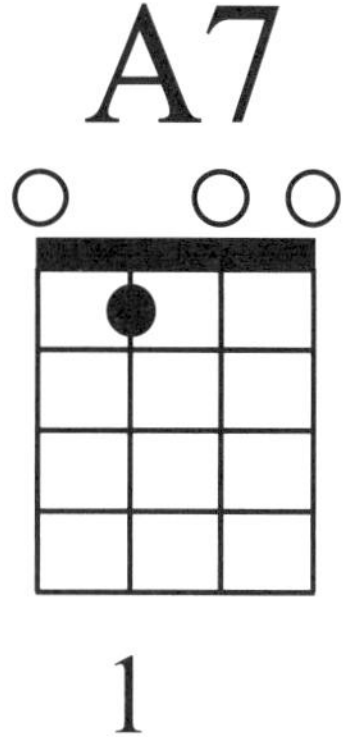

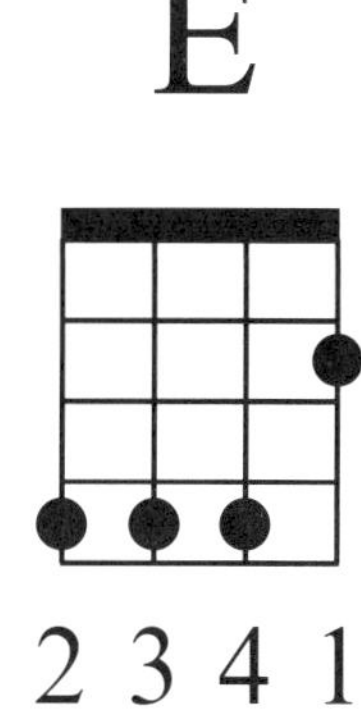

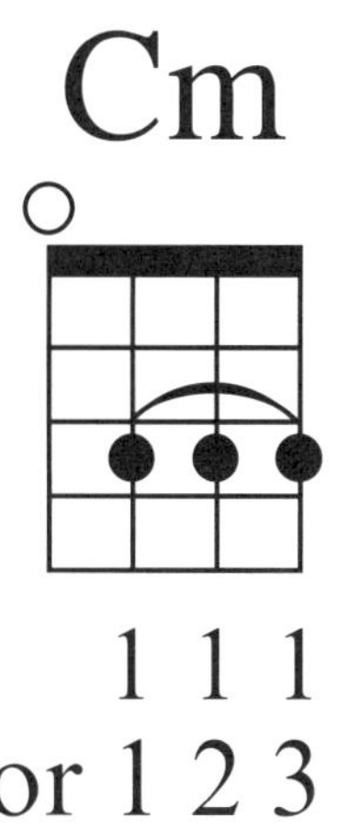

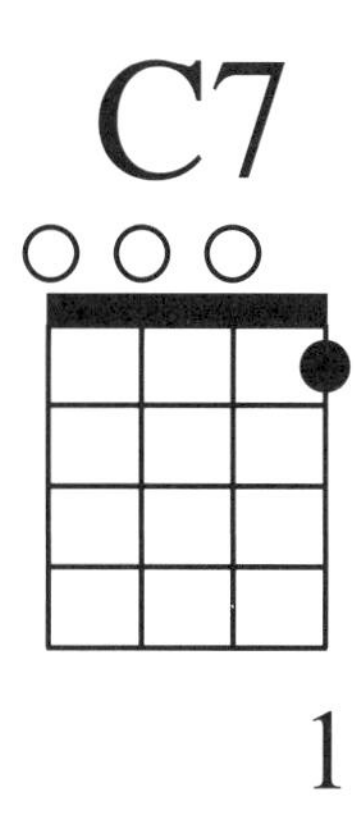

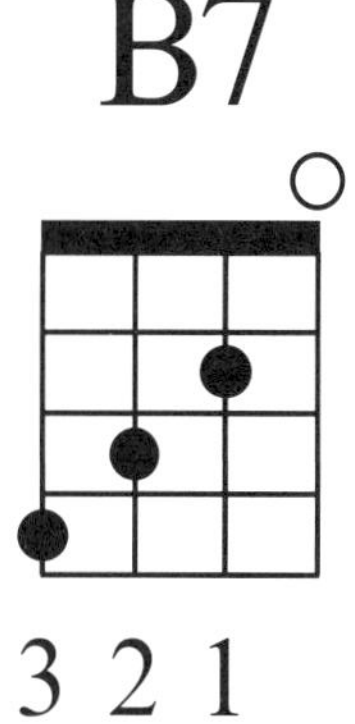

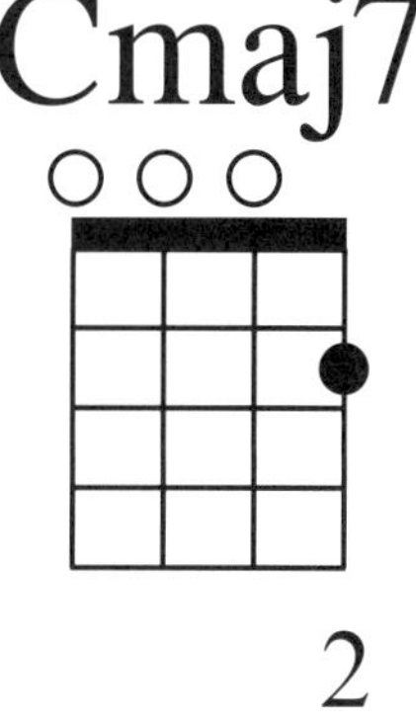

The Best Collections for Ukulele

The Best Songs Ever

70 songs have now been arranged for ukulele. Includes: Always • Bohemian Rhapsody • Memory • My Favorite Things • Over the Rainbow • Piano Man • What a Wonderful World • Yesterday • You Raise Me Up • and more.

00282413

Campfire Songs for Ukulele

30 favorites to sing as you roast marshmallows and strum your uke around the campfire. Includes: God Bless the U.S.A. • Hallelujah • The House of the Rising Sun • I Walk the Line • Wagon Wheel • You Are My Sunshine • and more.

00129170

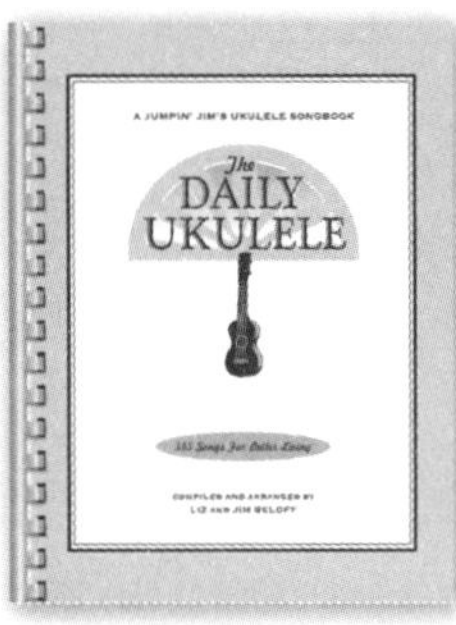

The Daily Ukulele

arr. Liz and Jim Beloff

Strum a different song everyday with easy arrangements of 365 of your favorite songs in one big songbook! Includes favorites by the Beatles, Beach Boys, and Bob Dylan, folk songs, pop songs, kids' songs, Christmas carols, and Broadway and Hollywood tunes, all with a spiral binding for ease of use.

00240356 Original Edition
00240681 Leap Year Edition
00119270 Portable Edition

Disney Hits for Ukulele

Play 23 of your favorite Disney songs on your ukulele. Includes: The Bare Necessities • Cruella De Vil • Do You Want to Build a Snowman? • Kiss the Girl • Lava • Let It Go • Once upon a Dream • A Whole New World • and more.

00151250

Also available:
00291547 Disney Fun Songs for Ukulele
00701708 Disney Songs for Ukulele
00334696 First 50 Disney Songs on Ukulele

First 50 Songs You Should Play on Ukulele

An amazing collec-tion of 50 accessible, must-know favorites: Hey, Soul Sister • I Walk the Line • I'm Yours • Imagine • Over the Rainbow • The Rainbow Connection • Riptide • and more.

00149250

Also available:
00292982 First 50 Melodies on Ukulele
00289029 First 50 Songs on Solo Ukulele
00347437 First 50 Songs to Strum on Uke

40 Most Streamed Songs for Ukulele

40 top hits that sound great on uke! Includes: Despacito • Feel It Still • Girls like You • Happier • Havana • High Hopes • The Middle • Perfect • 7 Rings • Shallow • Shape of You • Something Just like This • Stay • Sucker • Sunflower • Sweet but Psycho • Thank U, Next • Without Me • and more!

00298113

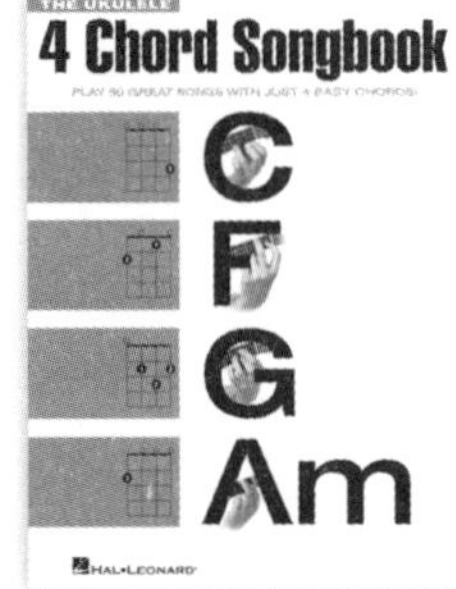

The 4 Chord Songbook

With just 4 chords, you can play 50 hot songs on your ukulele! Songs include: Brown Eyed Girl • Hey Ya! • Ho Hey • Jessie's Girl • Let It Be • One Love • Stand by Me • Toes • With or Without You • and many more.

00142050

Also available:
00141143 The 3-Chord Songbook

Pop Songs for Kids

30 easy pop favorites for kids to play on uke, including: Brave • Fight Song • Happy • Havana • House of Gold • How Far I'll Go • Let It Go • Rewrite the Stars • Roar • Shake It Off • What Makes You Beautiful • and more.

00284415

Simple Songs for Ukulele

50 favorites for standard G-C-E-A ukulele tuning, including: All Along the Watchtower • Can't Help Falling in Love • Don't Worry, Be Happy • Ho Hey • I'm Yours • King of the Road • Sweet Home Alabama • You Are My Sunshine • and more.

00156815

Also available:
00276644 More Simple Songs for Ukulele

Top Hits of 2022

This collection features 16 of today's top hits arranged with vocal melody, lyrics, and chord diagrams for standard G-C-E-A tuning for ukulele. Songs include: As It Was • Carolina • Enemy • Freedom • Glimpse of Us • Hold My Hand • Numb Little Bug • On My Way • and more.

01100312

Also available:
00355553 Top Hits of 2020
00302274 Top Hits of 2019

Ukulele: The Most Requested Songs

Strum & Sing Series
Cherry Lane Music

Nearly 50 favorites all expertly arranged for ukulele! Includes: Bubbly • Build Me Up, Buttercup • Georgia on My Mind • Your Body Is a Wonderland • and more.

02501453

The Ultimate Ukulele Fake Book

Uke enthusiasts will love this giant, spiral-bound collection of over 400 songs for uke! Includes: Crazy • Dancing Queen • Downtown • Fields of Gold • Happy • Hey Jude • 7 Years • Summertime • Thinking Out Loud • Thriller • Wagon Wheel • and more.

00175500 9" x 12" Edition
00319997 5.5" x 8.5" Edition

Order today from your favorite music retailer at halleonard.com

Prices, contents and availability subject to change without notice

Learn to play the

Ukulele

with these great Hal Leonard books!

Hal Leonard Ukulele Method

Book 1

by Lil' Rev

The Hal Leonard Ukulele Method is designed for anyone just learning to play ukulele. This comprehensive and easy-to-use beginner's guide by acclaimed performer and uke master Lil' Rev includes many fun songs of different styles to learn and play. The accompanying audio contains 46 tracks of songs for demonstration and play along. Includes: types of ukuleles, tuning, music reading, melody playing, chords, strumming, scales, tremolo, music notation and tablature, a variety of music styles, ukulele history and much more.

00695847 Book Only
00695832 Book/Online Audio
00320534 DVD

Book 2

00695948 Book Only
00695949 Book/Online Audio

Ukulele Chord Finder

00695803 9" x 12"
00695902 6" x 9"
00696472 Book 1 with Online Audio + Chord Finder

Ukulele Scale Finder

00696378 9" x 12"

Easy Songs for Ukulele

00695904 Book/Online Audio
00695905 Book

Ukulele for Kids

00696468 Book/Online Audio
00244855 Method & Songbook

Baritone Ukulele Method

00696564 Book/Online Audio

Bass Ukulele Method

00350667 Book/Online Audio

Jake Shimabukuro Teaches Ukulele Lessons

Learn notes, chords, songs, and playing techniques from the master of modern ukulele! In this unique book with online video, Jake Shimabukuro will get you started on playing the ukulele. The book includes full transcriptions of every example, the video features Jake teaching you everything you need to know plus video of Jake playing all the examples.

00320992 Book/Online Video

Fretboard Roadmaps – Ukulele

The Essential Patterns That All the Pros Know and Use

by Fred Sokolow & Jim Beloff

Take your uke playing to the next level! Tunes and exercises in standard notation and tab illustrate each technique. Absolute beginners can follow the diagrams and instruction step-by-step, while intermediate and advanced players can use the chapters non-sequentially to increase their understanding of the ukulele. The audio includes 59 demo and play-along tracks.

00695901 Book/Online Audio

Play Ukulele Today!

A Complete Guide to the Basics

by Barrett Tagliarino

This is the ultimate self-teaching method for ukulele! Includes audio with full demo tracks and over 60 great songs. You'll learn: care for the instrument; how to produce sound; reading music notation and rhythms; and more.

00699638 Book/Online Audio
00293927 Book 1 & 2/Online Media

Ukulele Aerobics

For All Levels, from Beginner to Advanced

by Chad Johnson

This package provides practice material for every day of the week and includes an online audio access code for all the workouts in the book. Techniques covered include: strumming, fingerstyle, slides, bending, damping, vibrato, tremolo and more.

00102162 Book/Online Audio

Do-It-Yourself Ukulele

The Best Step-by-Step Guide to Start Playing

by Terry Carter

Learn ukulele on your own terms with this incredibly helpful book. *Do-It-Yourself Ukulele* uses well-known pop, rock, blues, traditional, and Hawaiian tunes in its step-by-step instructions on what you need to know to get started and sounding like a pro in no time.

00359771 Book/Online Media

www.halleonard.com

Prices, contents and availability subject to change without notice.
Prices listed in U.S. funds.

1123
424